47

JOTTINGS IN A
GENERAL'S
NOTEBOOK

By the same author

TROOPING THE COLOUR
A History of the Sovereign's Birthday Parade

JOTTINGS IN A
GENERAL'S
NOTEBOOK

MICHAEL GOW
SCOTS GUARDSMAN

ENLISTED AS A GUARDSMAN 1942
RETIRED AS A GENERAL 1986

SOUVENIR PRESS

ISBN 0 285 62938 7

Photoset, Printed and Bound by WBC Ltd
Bristol and Maesteg

Acknowledgements

The illustrations of the Privy Council Room at Osborne House where these first jottings were made, and of the Duke of Cambridge, are reproduced by gracious permission of Her Majesty The Queen.

I am especially grateful to Tessa Harrow of Souvenir Press for her advice, suggestions and patience through the stages that my faltering memories passed, and to Penny Lewis without whose typing skills and, more importantly, ability to decypher my writing, the book would never have been produced.

I thank the following for allowing me to quote from published material: Macmillan Publishing Company, New York, for *A King's Story* (Copyright © 1951) by HRH The Duke of Windsor, published by Cassell & Co; Peters, Fraser and Dunlop for *Memoirs* by Lord Chandos, published by the Bodley Head; George Philip Ltd for *The Story of the Guards* by Lt. Col. Sir Julian Paget, published by Osprey; The Lady Anne Bentinck and the Welbeck Estates Company Ltd for *Men and Women and Things*, Memories of the Duke of Portland, published by Faber & Faber; John Murray (Publishers) Ltd for *Records and Reactions* by the Earl of Middleton; Century Hutchinson Ltd for *Notes of a Nomad* by Lady Jephson; Constable Publishers for *The Royal George* by Giles St Aubyn; Macmillan London for *Recollections of Three Reigns* by Sir Federick Ponsonby; Pillans & Wilson Specialist Litho Printers Ltd for *The History of the Royal Company of Archers* by Ian Hay, published by William Blackwood.

I would also like to thank Major General Lord Michael Fitzalan Howard for allowing me to quote extracts from a letter to him by the late Sir Iain Moncreiffe of that Ilk; the Duke of Atholl for permission to reproduce the correspondence between myself and the Adjutant, The Atholl Highlanders; and Captain Sir Iain Tennant, (Lieutenant of the Queen's Body Guard for Scotland, The Royal Company of Archers), for his permission to reproduce the Alex-Monty letters.

I am grateful to the following for allowing me to publish photographs and illustrations: The Estate of Sir Osbert Lancaster and John Murray (Publishers) Ltd for seven cartoons previously published in *Liquid Assets*, *Signs of the Times*, *Lady Littlehampton and Friends*, *Private Views* and *Tableaux Vivants*; Express Newspapers plc for three cartoons by Giles; Newspaper Publishing plc, the Imperial War Museum, RHQ Scots Guards, Captain David Bankes, George Outram & Co Ltd, The Scotsman Publications Ltd, Central Press/Photo Source, the Atholl Highlanders, and the Public Relations Photo Sections of HQ 4 Div and HQ BAOR.

Finally, I would like to thank my friends and acquaintances without whose help, wittingly or unwittingly, this book could not have been written. I hope I have insulted none but maybe amused some. My philosophy has always been that life *must* be fun, despite inevitable setbacks and transient sadnesses, and that *people* are important because it is they who can make or not make it so.

Contents

Preface

These Jottings were made in the Council Room at Osborne House, Queen Victoria's home in the Isle of Wight.

Sir Frederick (Fritz) Ponsonby in his book *Recollections of Three Reigns*, wrote:

(It) was Mid-Victorian in decoration, and some of the rooms were quite startling in their ugliness. Lord Rosebery once said that he thought the drawing room was the ugliest room in the world till he saw the drawing room at Balmoral . . . At noon the Queen went out and all the Members of the Household went for a walk, but it was like a lunatic asylum as everybody went alone in different directions . . . At three the Queen went out driving and again all the Members of the Household went walking by themselves.[1]

The Council Room, however, is beautiful, and from the desk by the window the distant Solent shimmers in the sunlight. It is steeped in history: In 1862, when Princess Alexandra paid her first visit to the Queen, accompanied by her father, Prince Christian of Denmark, the three dined here with Princess Helena. In 1898, one evening after dinner, Professor Bell demonstrated to the Queen for the first time the telephone, which was in communication with Osborne Cottage, no more than a quarter of a mile away, so by no

[1] *Recollections of Three Reigns*. Sir Frederick Ponsonby. Macmillan London.

stretch could he call it 'long distance'. And on 24 January, 1901, the new King, Edward VII, held a levee here at which all the members of the late Queen's Household were formally presented and kissed hands.

Where these jottings were recalled and recorded: the Privy Council Room, Osborne House, photographed by Disderi in 1867. *Copyright Reserved. Reproduced by gracious permission of Her Majesty The Queen*

The very atmosphere of the place, as I sat there, was conducive to recalling incidents from the past, covering forty-four years as a Guardsman (and beyond), almost every moment of which I have enjoyed. This is not an autobiography, but I have grouped these jottings in some rough, logical sequence with a brief introduction to each section for the benefit of the reader. I have started, however, with some general anecdotes, about the Foot Guards and Household Division, an organisation to which my life has been devoted in Service of the Sovereign.

'Chips' Maclean, to whom this book is dedicated, has always enjoyed the humorous things in Life, and has always been ready to contribute. The following is typical of the sort of anecdote that amused us both: T. S. Eliot, the poet, one evening stopped a taxi in London. As he got in, the cabby said, 'You're T. S. Eliot.' When asked how he knew, he replied, 'Ah, I've got an eye for a celebrity. Only the other evening I picked up Bertrand Russell, and I said to him, "Well, Lord Russell, what's it all about?" and do you know, he couldn't tell me!'

I met him once emerging from the old Guards Club in Charles Street, carrying an impressive briefcase. 'What have you got in there?' I asked.

'Very important papers,' he replied.

'I don't believe you. I bet it's just got a few dry cough drops in it,' and we opened it up, and I was right!

Time passed, and I happened to be walking in front of Buckingham Palace when I noticed a large crowd gazing through the railings and an enormous Royal Standard flying on the roof. There was 'Chips', walking in the other direction, with his briefcase.

'Hello,' I said, 'what's happening?'

'Oh, don't you know?' he replied. 'The Queen has had a son.'

'How splendid,' I said. 'Wouldn't it be nice if in that old briefcase of yours, instead of those cough drops, there was a bottle of the Liquid Amber so that we could toast His Royal Highness!' 'Chips' opened the case: there was and, there and then, we did!

13

1
The Guards

Writing of his experiences as an officer in the Grenadier Guards in the First World War:

'The Guards Division were the Shock Troops of the British Army; their prestige was purchased in blood.'

HRH The Duke of Windsor[1]

Time and again the Brigade of Guards have proved a bulwark in battle; time and again they have made the reputation of Commanders; always they have set a standard at which to aim and which, though sometimes equalled, is never surpassed.

Lord Chandos[2]

It is natural to expect higher standards from Guards Regiments and they have more than lived up to these expectations. Viewed with a mixture of envy and awe by the rest of the Army, they have never failed to provide a yardstick of excellence in every department, be it turn out drill, smartness, loyalty, courage or sacrifice. With a self confidence bred of success and a never failing attention to detail and professional competence, they have

[1] *A King's Story.* Cassell, 1951, p. 120.
[2] *Memoirs.* Bodley Head, 1962, p. 36.

weathered ridicule and adulation, malice and envy through all the changing fortunes of war and peace.

HRH the Duke of Edinburgh[1]

The Household Division comprises two Regiments of Household Cavalry—The Life Guards and The Blues and Royals—and five Regiments of Foot Guards—Grenadier, Coldstream, Scots, Irish and Welsh Guards.

They are a National Institution, and the personal Guards of the Sovereign, who is Colonel-in-Chief of each Regiment. Their responsibilities are to carry out the ceremonial duties which are a part of the outward sign of the Queen's Majesty, and to be fully trained operational soldiers. Thus they are to be found in the latter role serving in tanks and armoured cars, as infantry, parachutists and in the Special Air Service (or SAS).

The following jottings show different facets of some of the personalities in this unique organisation.

[1] Foreword to *The Story of the Guards*, Lt. Col. Sir Julian Paget. Osprey, 1976.

AN OLD GUARDSMAN

In 1878 Colonel Freemantle was in the chair at a meeting of the Coldstream Guards Officers' Dining Club,[1] and proposed a toast to the oldest Coldstreamer in the room—Lord Stradbroke, who in his reply said: 'I am also very proud to have been present with the Regiment at the famous battle of Quatre Bras, but unfortunately I was wounded and so was unable to be present at the much more famous battle the following day—I mean the battle at which the great Duke of Wellington commanded the Allied Army when it defeated the French under the Emperor Napoleon. But,' said Lord Stradbroke, 'you must excuse a temporary lapse of memory by an old man, for I cannot remember its name.' Someone said, 'Waterloo.' 'Waterloo —of course, Waterloo! How foolish of me not to remember.'

Remembered by the Duke of Portland, who was present.[2]

INITIATIVE

'Always show initiative,' remarked Colonel the 12th Earl of Stair, and by way of illustration related this tale: When he was a young officer serving with the Scots Guards at Windsor, he went on leave to his home at Stranraer. There he received a telegram from the Adjutant ordering his immediate return as the Major General was inspecting the Battalion the next day.

---

[1] Called the 'Nulli Club', after the motto of the Regiment: *Nulli Secundus* (Second to None).
[2] *Men and Women and Things*, Memories of the Duke of Portland. Faber & Faber, 1937.

17

He travelled south on the night train, took a hansom cab and, spurred on by the promise of a generous tip, the cabby galloped to Paddington, where to his horror he saw the Windsor train departing with the Major General and his staff on board.

He then remembered that a 'Special' was kept with steam up in case Queen Victoria summoned a Cabinet Minister to see her. He gave the Station Master his name and requirement, ran to the ticket office and wrote out a cheque (£5 for the Special, 2/6 for his ticket). Back he ran, jumped in, down went the flag, 'toot' went the whistle and the train departed. Because it was a 'Special', the line was cleared. The Major General was shunted into a siding as 2/Lieutenant the Lord Stair rattled past and arrived first.

SOME SAYINGS OF OF HRH PRINCE GEORGE, DUKE OF CAMBRIDGE

Born 1819, died 1904. Son of Adolphus, brother of Edward Duke of Kent, he was Queen Victoria's first cousin. He commanded a

"Tell me, Lionel – your French is better than mine – what exactly is a coup d'état?" Cartoon by Osbert Lancaster from *Liquid Assets. Reproduced by permission of The Estate of Sir Osbert Lancaster and John Murray (Publishers) Ltd*

18

Division in the Crimean War and was Commander-in-Chief of the Army 1856-1895, and Colonel Grenadier Guards 1861-1904. He married Louisa Fairbrother, an actress, on 8 January, 1847, who became 'Mrs FitzGeorge' by whom he had three sons. Whether Queen Victoria ever received her is uncertain. The Duke was loath to accept change but was regarded in the Army with respect and, latterly, with affection.

*   *   *

On reviewing all three battalions of the Grenadier Guards in Hyde Park: 'In all my experience of reviews in England, Ireland or on the Continent of Europe, I have never witnessed such a damnable exhibition of incompetence as has been shown by the Grenadier Guards today. When the Cease Fire was sounded, the First Battalion was firing at the Serpentine, the Second Battalion was firing at the Marble Arch, and God Almighty knows where the Third Battalion was firing. I don't.'[1]

On a parade, he was storming against the habit of swearing in the Army. 'I was talking it over with the Queen last night, and Her Majesty says she is damned if she will have it.'[2]

'Where are the pioneers?' he asked a Battalion Commanding Officer, 'I don't see them.' 'In front of the leading company, Your Royal Highness.' 'Have they got their picks and shovels with them?' 'Certainly, Your Royal Highness. Do you want them to do anything?' 'Yes,' said the Duke. 'I want them to dig a very deep and very wide hole and then bury this battalion in it.'[3]

At a dinner party given by a District Commander and attended (as the Duke well knew) by staff officers, most of whom had been to the Staff College: 'I am glad to know, Sir, that you

---

[1] *Records and Reactions.* The Earl of Middleton. John Murray, 1939, pp. 81-2.
[2] *Notes of a Nomad.* Lady Jephson. Hutchinson, 1918, pp. 177-8.
[3] *The Royal George.* Giles St Aubyn. Constable, 1963, p. 121.

HRH The Duke of Cambridge in the uniform of Colonel Grenadier
Guards, *c.* late 1890s. *Copyright reserved. Reproduced by gracious permission
of Her Majesty The Queen*

have no Staff College Officers on your staff. I don't like Staff College Officers. My experience of Staff College Officers is that they are conceited, and that they are dirty! Brains! I don't believe in brains. You haven't any, I know, Sir, and as for my Military Secretary over on the other side of the table, and a damned good Military Secretary too, he's the very stoopidest man I ever came across.'[1]

THE QUEEN'S HOSPITAL VISIT

Queen Victoria was devoted to her Army and to the Household Troops in particular. She was, moreover, extremely conscientious in visiting her soldiers in hospital. On one occasion, it is said, on entering a very full ward, she remarked to the Commanding Officer in attendance, 'What is that peculiar smell?' to which the reply came, 'That, Ma'am, is what we call in the Service "Esprit de Corps".'

GOLD STICK—THE 'HENCHMAN'

When Major General Lord Michael Fitzalan Howard[2] was appointed Colonel of The Life Guards and Gold Stick to the Queen, he received a letter from Sir Iain Moncreiffe of that Ilk, Bt, Albany Herald, dated 'St Fintan's Day 1980'. The following is an *extract* from that letter, which will also help the reader to

---

[1] *Stray Recollections.* Sir C. Callwell. Edward Arnold, 1923, Vol 1, p. 289.
[2] Scots Guards 1938. Major General Commanding the Household Division 1968-71. Marshal of the Diplomatic Corps 1972-81.

understand why Prince Edward of Saxe-Weimar[1] was so pleased when he was appointed to that office:

In 1953 the late and great Sir Thomas Innes of Learney, the Lord Lyon King of Arms, consulted me about the functions of Gold Stick. I explained that his job is the *immediate* and *personal* protection of the Sovereign's person—like the detective in attendance with an armpit holster filled and ready; that Silver Stick's job is back-up man to Gold Stick (who may be elderly and need to pop off for a moment if taken short unexpectedly) . . . Lyon pondered this opinion, then he exclaimed in his archaic Court Scots voice, 'I see. Gold Stick is the *Henchman*.'

With us, every Highland Chief had, as the principal officer in his 'tail', a tough and trusty right hand man—literally so, for he stood at his right hand—called 'the Henchman', whose duty it was to bash with lightning speed anybody who durst draw a weapon or strike the Chief. He was in fact, *the* Body Guard in person and *par excellence* . . . it is the Household Cavalry Gold Stick in Waiting whose sole duty is to be the Henchman with an eagle eye, quick on the draw (with his back up Tough—Silver Stick). So it is *you*, if in waiting, whom I will hold *primarily* responsible . . . Moreover, and this is the gist, She couldn't be entrusted to better hands. Long may you be the Henchman.

A SENSE OF OCCASION

The Duke of Portland recalled in his Memoirs that at one of his banquets General Prince Edward of Saxe-Weimar, who had lately been appointed Colonel of one of The Life Guards Regiments (an appointment which carried with it the office of Gold Stick), came rather early:

[1] Nephew of Queen Victoria. Born 1823. Ensign Grenadier Guards 1841 and served in the Crimean War with the 3rd Battalion. Major General Commanding the Brigade of Guards 1870-76. Colonel the 1st Life Guards (and Gold Stick) 1888-1902. Died 1902.

I therefore said, 'I'm afraid some of my guests haven't arrived yet so I hope you will sit down, Sir, till they come.' 'Sit Down? Sit down? Certainly not,' said Prince Edward. 'I shall only sit down once, and that will be at dinner. I'm very proud of my appointment and my new uniform. I saw myself in the glass just now, and by God! I thought I looked damn handsome. Sit down? Certainly not! I want everybody to see me.'[1]

The Prince was known to his contemporaries as 'dear old Fuddlediboo' or 'Fuddles' because, whenever he was excited, he began whatever he had to say with something like 'Fud-fud-fud'.

TWO ROYAL HOSPITAL VIGNETTES

Drum Major Everett, Scots Guards, was for some time before his death an In-Pensioner at the Royal Hospital, Chelsea. Talking of his time in the Regiment, he was asked if, when he married, he was allotted a Quarter. His reply was interesting: Yes, he was. He and his wife lived in one end of the barrack room and Mrs Everett did the washing for the soldiers. The couple were separated from the rest by a string across the room from which were suspended blankets. This may well be the origin of the expression 'the wrong side of the blanket'.

* * *

In his address at Founder's Day Parade, the Governor of the Royal Hospital said that an In-Pensioner aged over 80 was going to attend the D-Day anniversary celebrations in Normandy. The BBC heard of this and sent a reporter to interview him.

[1] *Men and Women and Things*, Memories of the Duke of Portland. Faber & Faber, 1937.

Photo Newspaper Publishing plc

What do you remember about D-Day?' he was asked.

'Nothing at all,' came the reply.

Somewhat taken aback, the interviewer then asked, 'Well, what are you going to do when you get over there?'

'Find myself a nice French girlfriend!' answered the Veteran.

AN UNEXPECTED APPOINTMENT

This story is confirmed by the present Lord Granard as being believed in the family.

The appointment of Master of the Horse was once a political one, and in 1907 the Earl of Sefton, who held that post, resigned because he could not support the Government over the Land Bills before Parliament that year.

The Earl of Granard was serving with the Scots Guards at the time and his brother officers thought they would play a practical joke on him. They despatched a telegram, purporting to come from the Prime Minister, inviting him to call at No. 10 Downing Street 'reference appointment as Master of the Horse'. Lord Granard was thrilled and showed the message to his friends before he set off.

The officers could hardly contain themselves as they awaited his return. 'Well,' they said, 'How did you get on?'

'Oh very well,' he replied, much to their dismay. 'There seemed to be a bit of a muddle at No. 10 as though I wasn't expected, but I soon cleared that up, showed the Private Secretary my telegram, and was shown in to the Prime Minister. He asked me about my politics—and, of course, I'm on his side—and whether I was a good horseman, which, as you chaps know, I am—and I got the job.'

And he had—and kept it from 1907 to 1915 and was reappointed 1924 to 1936.

The Earl of Granard, Master of the Horse, with (*left*) General the Earl of Cavan and (*right*) General Lord Allenby. *Reproduced by permission of the Imperial War Museum*

A DIRECTOR OF MUSIC'S GREATEST MOMENT

Captain F. W. Wood, MVO, joined the Army as a bandsboy, aged 14, in 1878. He was Director of Music, Scots Guards, from 1900 to 1929 and Senior Director of the Brigade of Guards from 1921. In 1921 he recalled: 'The greatest moment in my life was the occasion of the end of the Great War. I was hurriedly summoned by telephone from my home near Clapham Common to Buckingham Palace. The Bandsmen from the Brigade of Guards, who live all over London, were summoned by telephone and special messenger to the courtyard of the Palace.

'We gathered breathlessly together under the balconies.

Armistice Day, 11 November, 1918. The scene outside Buckingham Palace while the Band played in the Forecourt. *Reproduced by permission of the Imperial War Museum*

27

Outside the gates of the Palace the great, excited crowd was swelling every minute as hundreds more people poured along the Mall. They cheered and cheered, and the King and Queen with the Prince of Wales and Princess Mary appeared again and again on the balcony in response to their acclamations.

'I had no music but I got the bandmen to play anything and everything we could remember—such pieces as 'Tipperary', 'Keep the Home Fires Burning' . . . Somehow we got through that impromptu programme—but the harmony! We made some show of music, and the crowds alternately cheered and sang as the King and Queen returned to the balcony.

'Then the King sent for me. I went to his study and found him almost overcome with emotion. His Majesty thanked me for the performance, and enquired if the bandsmen were being looked after. I have never seen the King look so moved by anything as I saw him in his study that day.

'Outside in the corridor I met the Queen. She stopped me and thanked me. There were tears in Her Majesty's eyes as she spoke of the wonderful reception which the crowds had given their Sovereign.'

This must surely have been one of the most exceptional performances ever by the Massed Bands of the Foot Guards.

A LETTER TO THE TIMES

Sir Frederick (Fritz) Ponsonby was the son of Sir Henry Ponsonby who was for many years Private Secretary to Queen Victoria. Fritz was a distinguished courtier who served the Queen, Edward VII and George V in many appointments. He also wrote, not very successfully, film scripts and attempted to find the treasure lost by King John in the Wash (also unsuccessfully). While a stickler for etiquette, he was also a wit, as demonstrated by the following letter to *The Times* of 9 August, 1929:

Sir,

Whether it is from lack of imagination on the part of the College authorities, or a paucity of ideas on the part of the haberdashers, the fact remains that the Old Wykehamist tie, which to the best of my belief only sprang into existence of late years, resembles the Guards' and it so closely that expert students of haberdashery unaided by microscopes are unable to detect the difference, especially when it is somewhat faded. The Guards' tie is composed of the Royal colours, and this privilege was no doubt given to them as the Sovereign's Household troops, but it is difficult to understand what justification there is for the Old Wykehamists wearing the Royal colours in a faded condition.

Many years ago it was said that the tie of the Upper Tooting Bicycle Club was practically the same as the Guards' tie. If that club is still in existence the position must indeed be confusing, but perhaps a super-tie might be devised to denote those who, having been educated at Winchester, joined the Household Brigade and have not been subsequently black-balled from the Upper Tooting Bicycle Club.

Ponsonby was educated at Eton, had served in the Grenadiers and became the first Baron Sysonby.

REGIMENTAL SERGEANT MAJOR FREDDIE ARCHER

Freddie Archer retired from the Scots Guards and the Army as a Captain and Quartermaster, but it was as the Regimental Sergeant Major of the Training Battalion Scots Guards at Pirbright in the war that he was best known throughout the whole Army.

He had walked from Scotland in 1912 to enlist, working his way south from farm to farm, where he got casual work. He once recalled that when he joined, dinners were the same every day—roast beef, suet roll and custard, served onto a slab of bread on the table, as there were no plates, which was then scrubbed and Polystoned clean. Guardsmen 'walked out' in uniform and for a

Regimental Sergeant Major 'Freddie' Archer, Scots Guards. *By permission of RHQ Scots Guards*

day's pay of a shilling (old money), he said he could entertain a girlfriend as follows:

Two pints of beer	2d
Five Woodbine cigarettes	½d
Two fish and chips	2d
Two seats at the Victoria Palace	6d

That left 1½d which bought another pint for him and a half pint for the girlfriend.

When this legendary figure, who was highly decorated in World War I, became the Sergeant Major at Pirbright, it was said that he always saluted before speaking to an officer on the telephone, and once put himself on a charge for being late.

Freddie himself related this story of a young Guardsman whom he had known as a 'Boy' Soldier (in the technical sense):

He was in no sense a 'bad' boy but rather mischievous and generally a nuisance. One night in 1941 it was reported to me at about 2200 hours that Boy Withers had been found hanging from a bathroom door. On proceeding there I found Withers lying on the floor with some bootlaces tied round and hanging from his neck. Knowing him and sensing the affair was a very cleverly staged hoax, I ordered him to straighten his legs, close his heels and lie properly to attention. His reaction was instantaneous and natural. He was placed straight inside the guardroom in double time and I phrased his charge to read:

1 Extremely idle committing suicide at about 2200 hours—i.e. still breathing at 2215 hours.
2 Using Army bootlaces for an improper purpose.

He was a great Scots Guardsman and, as such, a perfectionist in all things!

31

AN ARREST OF DISTINCTION

Each stand of importance on Horse Guards Parade, erected for the Sovereign's Birthday Parade, is manned by an officer and two Non-Commissioned officers of the Foot Guards. Their job is to check tickets and to guide the holders to their seats.

On one occasion it so happened that the officer (a Coldstreamer) detailed to look after what he subsequently discovered was the Diplomatic Stand, was considerably put out. A stranger, wearing a transparent mackintosh over his morning coat, festooned with cameras, suddenly appeared and started to throw his weight about, directing people left and right. The officer had no idea who he was and told him to desist as it was nothing to do with him. The stranger paid not the slightest attention and continued to interfere, so the officer summoned a couple of police officers and asked them to remove the interloper who, he said, must be deranged. This they did and he was taken from sight through the Arch.

Twenty minutes later he reappeared, glared at the officer and took a seat in the stand. He was, it transpired, the Marshal of the Diplomatic Corps. The Ambassadors who had witnessed the incident were most amused!

A FIELD MARSHAL'S FUNERAL

The officer of the Foot Guards in charge of the Military Attachés at the funeral of Field Marshal Earl Alexander of Tunis, Colonel Irish Guards, had formed them up in a solid block in sixes and was still briefing them in some haste as the coffin, in silent dignity, was carried out of the gymnasium of the barracks in Windsor. Ringing out across the square were heard his final words: 'Regardless of Race, Religion or Politics, we step off with the left foot, but we keep our dressing by the right.'

His comment, on reflection was, 'I am sure Alex would have laughed even if the Major General did not.'

AN INSPECTION

Occasionally a Battalion of the Line helps out the Foot Guards with the Public Duties in London, and the Garrison Sergeant Major gives them invaluable help and advice. On one occasion, when such a Battalion was preparing for this duty, the Garrison Sergeant Major checked them over, and when he came to the Band, his eye fell upon the Bass Drummer who happened to come from an 'ethnic minority'. He was wearing a leopard skin. 'Who gave you permission to wear plain clothes?' commented the Sergeant Major.

"—— and finally, never forget that every man carries two volumes of memoirs and a field-marshal's syndication rights in his knapsack!" Cartoon by Osbert Lancaster from *Signs of the Times. Reproduced by permission of The Estate of Sir Osbert Lancaster and John Murray (Publishers) Ltd*

DRAWBACKS OF WINDSOR CASTLE

The Military Knights live in the Lower Ward, and each house has a small front garden. 'Dusty', a distinguished Scots Guards Quartermaster, is a Knight, and to mark his 80th birthday the Major General Commanding the Household Division held a luncheon in his honour. Sitting on his right:

'It must be very nice, living in the Castle?'

'Oh yes. In the summer, though, the tourists muck it up. Came out of my front door one morning and there on my lawn was a Japanese family, picnicking. "Would you please leave." Not a move. "Oh p*** off!" They left like a shot. My neighbour heard this altercation: "My word, Dusty, I never knew you spoke Japanese!"'

'Dusty' (alias Major H. Smith, MBE, Military Knight) outside his home in the Lower Ward of Windsor Castle.

TEA WITH A MILITARY KNIGHT

I arranged to call upon the same Military Knight, and he was kind enough to invite me to tea, which he had set out beautifully. The pile of sandwiches quickly disappeared and a pile of cakes was then produced.

'I made these myself, y'know,' he said.

'Really! I knew that you were a man of many abilities but I never knew you could cook.'

'Oh yes,' he said, 'tuck in.' I did so, removing from the first cake the paper surrounding it. It was delicious.

'Marvellous, Dusty, but do tell me, why have you written "Lyons" on the bottom of each?' For once my host was at a loss as to how to reply!

A PIPING COMMENT

The Prime Minister (Harold Wilson) was staying at Balmoral as the Queen's guest. He picked up the programme of pipe music to be performed after dinner, and seeing 'The 78th's Farewell to Gibraltar', remarked to Her Majesty, 'Don't worry, Ma'am, it will never happen.' Whereupon the Officer Commanding the Ballater Guard (furnished by the Scots Guards) pointed to another tune on the programme and said, 'But, Prime Minister, what about that?' The tune was 'The Barren Rocks of Aden', which was about to be given up.

A PIPING PROBLEM

In the Scots Guards, the Picquet Officer—known in the Infantry of the Line as the Orderly Officer—presides at a formal dinner in the Officers' Mess. He may be the most junior and newly joined

35

officer, and one of his duties is to tell the Piper, who plays after dinner, marching round the table, the tunes for the second 'set' (or programme). Normally this comprises a Quick March, Strathspey, Reel and a final March. There is often considerable discussion amongst the officers as to what tunes he should play, but at last the Picquet Officer leaves the room, desperately trying to recall the chosen titles.

On one such occasion, when he went out the luckless officer found to his horror that his mind was a complete blank. In desperation he said to the Piper, 'For Heaven's sake. Play something jolly!'

2
Anecdotes of Family and School

My maternal Grandmother died tragically and young, and in consequence my Mother and Aunt were brought up by a Nanny who later also largely brought up my brother and myself. She was a remarkable woman, full of wisdom which she imparted to us from an early age. 'The art of conversation,' I remember she once told us, 'lies not in what you say but in how you observe and *listen*. Make the person who is talking with you believe that what he or she is saying is the most important thing you have ever heard.'

I have put together, as Nanny exhorted, things that I have seen or heard which have nothing to do with my time as a soldier but which have stayed in my memory over the years—and maybe contributed to my personality.

None of my forebears were military men—they were artists, musicians and above all academics. Had it not been for Hitler, I might well have become a professor: I rather fancied myself shuffling across a university quadrangle, hot-footing it to the Senior Commonroom. Stories of schools and schoolmasters have always therefore appealed to me, and so I have also included some appropriate jottings.

A CORONATION INCIDENT

When the coronation of King Edward VII was being planned, procedures and 'rights' were in doubt as there had been no previous similar event for 64 years. A Court of Claims was set up before which claimants of rights and privileges had to establish their case.

The Headmaster of Westminster School (Dr Gow) presented his case, which was confirmed, that the King's scholars of his school should be present in the Abbey—and their salutation 'Vivat Regina Alexandra, Vivat Rex Edwardus' was woven into the Coronation Music by Sir Hubert Parry.

The Headmaster, however, went a step further. Towards the end of the service, at the moment when the King reappeared from the Chapel of the Confessor, he called on his Westminster boys for three cheers for His Majesty. An eye witness, Bishop Handley Moule, recorded 'the response, strange as it may seem to cheer in church, sounded majestic as we listened from the Chapel—long waves of echoing sound.' Fortunately the King approved. Today the Headmaster would surely be seized by the police and forcibly ejected.

A MOMENT NEVER TO BE FORGOTTEN

The day that World War I ended, the same Headmaster of Westminster assembled the whole school. 'Boys,' he declared, 'today is an historic occasion, and one which you will never forget all your lives. There are some who think that I will award a half holiday; there may be some who think I will award a whole holiday. Both are wrong. Work will continue as usual, and that is why you will never forget today.'

38

This story was clearly remembered in 1976 by an old man who was present on that occasion.

GRANDFATHER

My maternal grandfather was a remarkable man. He never had a meal in any house other than his own because he was sure that the food would be disgusting, and if he ever accepted an invitation from a friend to go and have a drink, he always took the precaution of having one or two before he left home in case that offered by his host was below his accustomed standard.

When I was quite young, I often sat with him in his study, when occasionally he would give me advice about Life. 'Always remember,' he once said, 'beware of a woman who wears a yellow dress.' Most of the time, however, we sat in companionable silence. Even in summer there was a fire going in the grate, and I recall him suddenly saying to me, 'Mike, ring the bell,' which I did and sat down again. Some minutes passed, and then the door opened. 'You rang, sir?' asked the servant. 'Yes,' he replied, 'put a lump of coal on the fire'—and even at that age I wondered why he couldn't have put it on himself.

Almost my last memory of this grey bearded and kindly man was sitting beside him by the sea. 'It's a sad thing but at my age my eyesight isn't what it was,' he remarked, and I pictured him with a white stick, walking with me arm in arm. But a few minutes later he suddenly said, 'That's a very fine looking woman over there!'

A LEFT WING VIEW OF PUBLIC SCHOOLS

The late Lord George Brown began an after luncheon address as follows:

39

'I'll start by telling you something that irritates some of my political colleagues. I'm Governor of a Public School—a *proper* Public School; not like that wishy-washy liberal school, Eton. And what's that Communist place? Ah yes, Winchester!'

PARENTS

They came down to see their boy during his first term at Public School and were walking along a street by his House when he said suddenly, 'Watch it, here come some of our chaps. Don't do anything peculiar.'

A CRICKETING MOTHER

My mother lived in a flat near Lord's Cricket Ground where she was a regular attendant, with rover tickets liberally supplied by friends. At one Test Match she espied two clergymen forlornly queuing in the hope of getting in to one of the public stands. She took pity on them and not only gave them tickets but also asked them back for lunch. While drinking a glass of preprandial sherry, she said, 'This must be a useful occasion for you both to refer to in a future sermon.' They looked mystified. 'Yes,' she continued, 'it's a first class miracle: seats at Lord's and lunch with me!'

She was a keen performer in her youth and once hit a ball so square to leg that ball and bat ended up in the wicket keeper's mouth.

Despite her knowledge of the game, my brother and I were mortified by her when she was umpiring a match. There was an appeal for LBW to which she replied. 'In.' (Somewhat like an appeal against a ducal batsman. The umpire was his butler who answered, 'Beg pardon, not in, Your Grace.')

MOTHER GOES TO WAR

Mother was one of the first women members of the Edinburgh City Police, which she joined in the spring of 1939. Whether she was in the Criminal Investigation Department or something more menial, such as Catering, she never revealed, but at least she was in a position to tell the family, several days before ordinary folk knew, that war was about to be declared, which was impressive and definitely suggested an appointment of importance.

When HMS *Hood* was sunk, she immediately packed a case and departed for London. She went to the Admiralty and demanded to see one of Their Lordships. Who she in fact saw is not recounted but she said, 'The country is in grave danger and I have come to join the Women's Royal Naval Service (WRNS).

Mother goes to War, Edinburgh, September 1939. The family said that if Hitler had seen this picture he would never have started the war. *She* said it was all because he had never played cricket — nor had Mussolini, for that matter.

41

Naturally I shall expect to be commissioned at once and employed on very secret work with a high-up Admiral.'

The officer whom she thus addressed was somewhat taken aback: 'Why do you think that you are suited to work of that nature?'

'Don't be impertinent, young man,' she replied, 'I do *The Times* Crossword puzzle every day.'

She could never understand why she was not accepted—and joined the Red Cross instead.

A CONFESSION

The don was an ardent member of a religious Group, one of whose tenets is absolute honesty. Accordingly one day he said to a fellow don:

'Spare me a minute, please, I have a confession to make to you.'

'Not now, I'm a bit pushed.'

'It can't wait. I simply *must* tell you. It is unbearable for me if I don't.'

'Well another time, if you must—try tomorrow.'

'No,' he cried, 'it must be *now*. It's about your wife. I have harboured terrible thoughts about her!' This put his fellow don off even more, but the Grouper was insistent.

'Just say you are sorry and we'll forget the whole thing.'

'No. I must tell you it *all*. It was last Sunday in Chapel. My eyes fell on your wife.'

'Say no more.'

'I must! I must! As I gazed at her, I had this *terrible thought:* By God! I've never seen such an ugly woman in my life!'

APPEARANCE IN COURT

Senior 'men', as boys at Winchester are called, were allowed to attend the Assizes, as part of their education, provided that the cases were considered not too improper.

On one such occasion the Clerk announced, 'The next charge, M'Lud, is in regard to a Carnal Case.' The 'men' woke up; the Judge cast upon them a searching glance and pursed his lips. 'The Accused, M'Lud, is charged with contravening the meat rationing regulations.' What a disappointment! His Lordship adjusted his wig, returned his gaze to the Wykehamical benches—and winked.

A HEADMASTER'S DESCRIPTION AND A PIECE OF ADVICE

Spencer Leeson, later Bishop of Peterborough, when Headmaster of Winchester, was once asked how he would describe a typical Old Wykehamist. He thought for a moment and then replied: 'He is the sort of man who would have a nervous breakdown doing the parish accounts.'

He also gave the following advice to a boy who was about to go out into the world at the end of his last half (or term): 'You will find that Life is not all full of tarts and cheesecake.'

THE PROFESSOR

There was once a senior professor at a College of Science who looked in appearance and mannerisms so eccentric as to be an improbable caricature of his profession.

One morning, on leaving for work, his wife said to him, 'Now don't forget we are moving today to another house in the campus. I've written the address down on this bit of paper and I'll put it in your pocket. All right—you won't forget, will you?' And off he went.

In the evening he returned home and to his surprise he couldn't get in to his house. He was even more astonished, when he peered through the windows, to see that there was no furniture within.

He wandered round aimlessly till he saw a child on a bicycle, whom he hailed. 'I am Professor _____,' he said, 'and I wonder if you can tell me what's happened to my house?'

'Don't be silly, Daddy,' replied the child. 'Follow me and I'll show you!'

A SCHOOLBOY'S REPLY

The Headmaster of a school for Scots children from Service backgrounds overheard a boy, whose father served in a Highland regiment, telling his friends: 'My dad was wounded in the leg in Northern Ireland, but as he fell he shot the IRA man who did it.' His audience was impressed.

After a pause, another boy, from another Highland regiment, not to be outdone, said, 'My dad was once stabbed in the arm with a knife.'

'Gracious me!' said the Head. 'Whoever did that?'

And the answer was, 'Mum!'

THE CLUB ENCOUNTER

I had arranged to meet my elder brother in the 'Senior', a club to which I did not belong. I arrived a little early and was shown into the smoking room by a club servant and asked to wait. The room was empty except for an old man who was sitting the other side of the fire, wearing what looked like Boy Scout's hat and reading a sporting journal. Silence prevailed until the senior member lowered his paper and looked across with watery eyes.

'Do you, perchance, play croquet (pronounced "crockett")?' he asked.

'I'm afraid not, sir,' I replied.

'Pity. Good game. It's not like tennis, y'know. All the balls are different colours.'

Up went the paper and silence was restored.

A VISIT TO THE TAILORS

'I think, sir, that as we haven't made a suit for you for a while, we should check your measurements. Step forward, Cyril.' Out came the tape and my vital statistics were checked and recorded.

When they came to the legs: '48; 53; 26pc—oh yes, *very* pc.'

'What's all this about "pc"?' I asked.

'Oh, nothing to worry about, sir,' I was told.

'But it's about my legs, isn't it?' I persisted.

'Just a term we use in the trade, sir.'

'But I *do* worry as it's about me! "Pc", indeed—and "very pc", too. What's it mean?'

Grudgingly, as if it were classified information, I was told: 'Prominent calf.'

COURTING DAYS

When, shortly after the end of World War II, I met my future wife, I found that Spanish was frequently spoken *en famille.* This was because she had been brought up in South America and had later joined her father in Madrid where he was on the Embassy staff. I often wondered what they were discussing as we sat round

45

My future wife, aged 13, in South America with a few of her friends.

Another reason why Hitler was defeated. My wife was a Leading Wren (Visual Signaller), and referred to by the President of the Royal British Legion Scotland as a 'War Veteran' — which is true.

the dining room table, not understanding a word, and sometimes thought it might be *me* ('Good heavens, this fellow's here again! What's he up to?' etc. etc.).

One evening we were both invited to a dance in a foreign Embassy where the food and drink were excellent. To my surprise, I was quite enjoying it all till a very smooth, dark haired man (possibly the Ambassador himself) whirled my fiancée away on to the dance floor. I noticed that he talked softly and incessantly to her as they gavotted around, and when he returned her to me eventually, I asked, 'That fellow never stopped talking! Whatever was he saying to you?'

'Oh, the usual things,' she replied.

'Usual things? What "usual things"?'

'Oh,' she said, 'like "I kiss your feet: your ears are like crushed coral petals . . ." '

'Crushed coral petals!' I gasped. 'That's it! We're off.' And off we went.

ON GETTING ENGAGED

My future wife took me, her fiancé, down to the West Country to meet her grandparents. Her grandfather was a Master of Foxhounds and after dinner he went into the hall where in those days the telephone was kept, and rang up his son.

'Well,' he shouted, 'We've got this feller here. Doesn't ride to hounds and I actually caught him reading a book! We've never had anyone like that in the family before. D'you think he's all right?'

A MOUNTED CHARGE

I was once in the State of Alberta, Canada, and learned that at Calgary was based the famous Regiment—Strathcona's Horse. I asked if I might call upon them. There was a special reason for this request: the grandfather of my wife, Major General Jack Seely, later First Lord Mottistone, had commanded in World War I the Canadian Cavalry Brigade, of which Strathcona's was a unit.

The Regiment had gone to immense trouble: there was a visit to their Museum, followed by a reception and a dinner. They had flown in from British Columbia a retired Lieutenant Colonel who remembered 'the General', as he called Jack Seely, extremely well. Indeed, he had been his trumpeter at the famous charge of the Canadian Cavalry Brigade at Moreuil Wood in March 1918, which has been described in many war histories and which halted the German Offensive at the time and place where it might have been decisive.

The Colonel, in his dinner speech, recalled his intimate association with General Seely:

'The General appreciated the urgency of action. He was mounted on his charger, Warrior, and he turned to me and said, "Sound the Charge." I lifted my trumpet to my lips and did so. The General, accompanied by me, his ADC and his lance bearer, galloped forward, with the whole brigade behind us. "Give us covering fire," he shouted, as we passed through our infantry, and up the hill towards Moreuil Wood we galloped . . .'

He was recalling a dramatic moment in history—maybe the last mounted cavalry charge in war—and when, in response, I said that not only had my wife *seen* Warrior but actually also *ridden* him, the Old Trumpeter was indeed deeply moved.

THE MOTHER-IN-LAW

My mother-in-law was a daughter of the only Privy Councillor and Member of Cabinet to have crewed a life boat. It was hardly surprising that she was a woman of great character and some eccentricity.

Once, when walking with her daughter and myself, she paused outside a striptease club and gazed at the photographs displayed. 'What pretty gels,' she remarked. 'I do hope they don't catch cold with so little on. There is a nasty nip in the air.'

On another occasion she accompanied her husband and six of her family to a musical show—*Oklahoma* or *Annie, Get your Gun.* The party sat in the middle of the third row of the stalls. About the second act, she suddenly rose and said very loudly, 'This show is disgusting! We will all leave.' The singers stopped, the orchestra stopped, members of the audience shouted, 'Shut up! Sit down!' But out we all went.

She was keen both on fresh air and 'clean' language. One day she said to me, 'There is a word I will not have said in my presence: it is a small word beginning with "s" and ending in "x".'

"What should I say, though,' I asked, 'if I have to use that word?'

She thought for a moment and replied, 'Hygiene.' She was not pleased later to hear me remark, 'I say, don't you think Brigitte Bardot is exceptionally hygienic!'

SPANISH EXPERIENCES

I considered my wife very knowledgeable about Spain and its language. I had assumed that she understood the customs; after all, she had actually lived there. I became slightly disillusioned, however, when we visited San Sebastian.

I had been instructed to go to a well known London emporium

49

to get suitably kitted out. The salesman assured me that a bright yellow sports shirt and *very* short shorts were just the thing, though I had my doubts. My wife made no comment, and on arrival she announced that we would go out and *passear*, which apparently was what the locals meant by a stroll.

We had hardly left the hotel before I sensed that something was wrong: people stopped in their tracks and pointed; windows were flung open and faces peered down; even a bus stopped and remarks were shouted at me, which naturally I did not understand and which my wife seemed to ignore.

And then I suddenly realised: I was unique. No Spanish man was dressed like me (and would not be seen dead in shorts in those days—and especially shorts like mine). And of course I was dressed in the Spanish national colours!

Some years later I managed to get my wife's services enlisted as an interpreter for a visit by an important Spanish delegation.

'Ah,' said the principal British official to her, 'please ask our visitors what their Government's attitude is to nuclear proliferation.' Don't be silly,' she replied, 'I don't even know what that means in English!'

Nevertheless she was fluent and, I was told, her accent was exquisite. I, on the other hand, after one entire term at school, could only say one phrase, which I told young officers to fit in to an entirely credible scenario. They failed. It was: 'Mrs Dolores has given me the purse. I will sleep peacefully.' Perhaps it was not surprising.

A FAMILY PICNIC

My wife decided that we would go for a picnic, so I loaded the boat with three children, food, drinks, cups, saucers, a brace of dogs, one cat, a table and camp chairs. Even this was a major achievement. Needless to say, the outboard engine was at its worst. Not only was it reluctant to start but when it did, frequently stalled. However, we eventually reached our destination on the river bank and the whole process of disembarkation took place, with little help from the children and positive hindrance from the animals. But it was completed and, utterly exhausted, I sank into a chair.

At that moment a boat passed us, and as it did so the woman on board was heard to say loudly to (presumably) her husband:

'Look at that'—pointing at my seated figure. 'Isn't that just typical! Dad taking it easy, as usual!'

"Dad, taking it easy — as usual."

LETTER TO CHEER UP A DAUGHTER AT SCHOOL

(Whose current interests were riding, racing and gnomes)

> Messrs Foghorn, Nozeband and Snaffle,
> Ornamental Gardeners,
> 'Timber Tops',
> Upton-on-the-Waddle,
> Surrey.

Dear Madam,

With reference to your esteemed order, we will be able to supply you with 2 dozen assorted gnomes at a favourable price. Each gnome is personally made under the supervision of my good Lady and no two are alike. In particular we recommend a special model which we call the 'Rustic Gnome'. He comes in various postures—horseback riding and showjumping on delightful pixie type 'horses'. The variety is quite delightful and, we find, extremely popular with the Nobility and Gentry.

We are not, strictly speaking, allowed to mention this and only do so in view of your esteemed custom, but a certain Royal Personage passed some extremely favourable comments on Mrs Foghorn's work and I have expectations of a large order for a new line, 'The Highland Gnome', to grace the purlieus of a Castle on Deeside.

I mention in closing that we also have a special 'run' of Military Gnomes, popular with retired Army Gentlefolk in Cheltenham. They can be clad in any type of uniform to taste. I have only last week despatched a considerable consignment of Scots Guards gnomes to a Colonel who must be nameless, but of impeccable taste. When they have been gracefully arranged in engaging postures about his sweeping acres, I shall be seeking his permission for my assistant, Mr Bert Higgins, to photograph the delightful spectacle for our brochure on this subject. In case you are interested, this will be published next month under the title 'Your garden is lacking if gnomeless'.

I remain, Madam, Your obedient Servant,

Alfred P Foghorn
Director

A BUNCH OF FLOWERS

I bought some flowers for my wife. I thought it would be a nice touch if I enclosed a card, and selected one from a rack in the shop. I asked if I could borrow a pen and, not having my spectacles with me, remarked to the salesgirl that it looked a pretty card.

'Oh yes,' she said. 'Will you want it delivered with the flowers direct to the undertaker?'

'Certainly not,' I replied, 'I shall deliver them direct to my wife. She's not dead and I hope she'll like these flowers.'

'Not with that card, she won't,' said the girl. 'It says "In Memoriam".'

WIFELY REMARKS

To an acquaintance: 'Oh yes, I think we met some time ago at that sailing place in Cowes.'

She was referring to the Royal Yacht Squadron, the senior and most prestigious yacht club in the realm, if not in the world.

*　　*　　*

53

Her late dog, a Yorkshire Terrier called Winkle, has a memorial tablet in the Dog's Cemetery, Edinburgh Castle.

To her husband: 'Don't speak to Winkle like that. She's *more* than human.'

* * *

She could have been in the *Guinness Book of Records.* The climax of the Military Tattoo was provided by over 600 musicians. They halted in front of the Salute Taker's box; the Director of Music worked them up into a *fortissimo* frenzy of sound; the spotlight fell on the General (myself) and his wife, who was sound asleep.

Later, on being admonished , all she said was, 'Well, anyhow, I never really liked military music!'

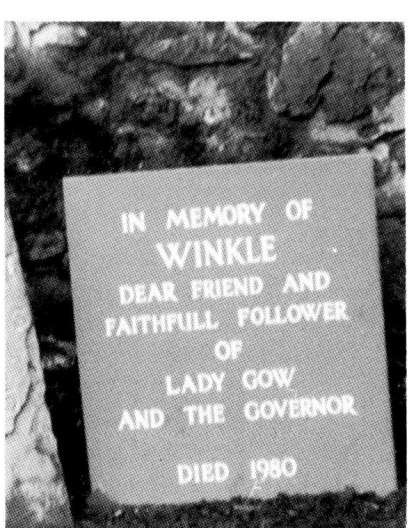

In Memoriam. The Dogs' Cemetery, Edinburgh Castle.

54

TIME AND THE WIFE

It was a constant struggle to get her to any event on time, because, she maintained, 'time is a figment of man's imagination'.

'Good heavens, we *must* be late,' a couple were heard to remark on arriving at a party. 'The Gows are here.'

A friend once said of her that she had a 'terrible fear of being punctual'.

Her trouble, however, was that she suffered from a disease known in the States as 'Threshold paralysis', particularly prevalent when saying 'Goodbye'.

A DRINK MISTAKEN

A charity concert was held in Highclere Castle, and during the interval the guests were allowed to wander around with a drink.

A friend of the late Lord Carnarvon introduced his wife to his host and left them together. With a glass in her hand she pointed to a picture and said, 'Isn't that Schneider, Lord Carnarvon?'

To which the reply came, 'Certainly not. It's the best champagne I could find.'

A DRINK DISGUISED

My wife was convinced that it was positively dangerous on the Continent to drink the water from a tap. Accordingly, in our house in Germany, she placed a bottle of Malvern water, which she had imported at considerable expense, in every bedroom. Guests were told, 'Don't drink the water. Malvern is the thing.'

I got so fed up paying for all this that I kept the bottles and refilled them from the tap. No one was ill, I saved money, and I only told her after two years!

MASTERMIND

A favourite TV programme of my wife is *Mastermind*. 'Granny's so riveted by it she ought to enter,' said one of the grandchildren.

'Oh no,' replied the other, 'She'd be hopeless. Magnus Magnusson would announce her and put her in the Hot Seat, and when he asked, "Occupation?" Granny would pause—and it would be *so* embarrassing—and answer, "Pass"!'

AN EMBARRASSING INCIDENT

I once took my family to a Horse Show in Germany. We picnicked, after which a female member announced that she wished to visit what the Americans call the 'Rest Room'.

This, it was discovered, was a tent, hanging from the pole of which was a printed notice which read, on one side, 'Vacant', and on the reverse, 'Engaged'. 'When you come out,' I said, 'do *not* forget to turn the notice round,' and with those words returned to my lunch where, in due course, she rejoined us.

Some time later a thought crossed my mind: 'Did you remember to do what I told you?' I asked. A slight, but it must be recorded as only 'slight', look of consternation crossed her face. I rose and peered through the hedge to see a queue of ladies waiting outside the tent! Who had to display moral courage and go and reverse the notice? It was *not* the miscreant!

A SHOOTING PARTY

The castle was grand and steeped in history; the Laird grandiose and eccentric. His butler struck an incongruous note: somehow one does not expect to hear a Jeeves with a cockney accent in the Highlands.

'Luverly day for the shoot, sir,' he remarked as he drew the bedroom curtains. "Course, Sir Edward doesn't 'ave 'em like in the old days. We 'ad some fun then, I can tell you. I remember, for instance, calling a young gentleman one mornin' like now. "I've laid out your shooting clothes, m'lord," I said—and 'e got the shock of 'is life, cos Sir Edward 'ad decided it would be fancy dress, and this gentleman 'ad to wear a suit of armour. Whoever was loadin' for 'im told me later 'e never 'it anything: every time a bird came over and 'e looked up 'is visor came down! Oh yes, we don't 'ave that now.'

BEFORE THE START OF A FUNERAL SERVICE

The Lord Lieutenant, whose voice was loud, said to a visitor sitting next to him, who happened to be a General and representing his family: 'We don't often have Generals to funerals here, y'know. Actually, now I come to think of it, we had one just before the Great War. He was representing the Army Council and came by train. When it stopped, the reception committee was waiting, but the General didn't alight, so they looked in the carriage window. What do you think they saw?'

'I've no idea.'

'The General was lying full length on the floor. What do you think had happened to him?'

'Drunk?'

'No, he'd been given a solid bronze wreath which he had put in the luggage rack. The train had stopped with a jerk: the wreath had fallen on his head and stunned him!'

At that moment the funeral procession arrived in the church.

3
The Guardsman, 1942

Strolling in the grounds of Winchester College was often seen the figure of an old and distinguished soldier who had been the Colonel of the Royal Scots. I got to know him quite well. 'Mark my words, my boy,' he said on one occasion, 'we're going to have trouble again with the Boche. And when that moment comes, make sure you join my Regiment—the 1st of Foot.' Being a Scot, this seemed to me good advice, and when war *was* declared (and I was $15\frac{1}{4}$) I at once wrote to the Commanding Officer of the Regimental Depot offering my services. He replied that the Army was not enlisting boy soldiers and so I could not join. Unperturbed I wrote again, applying to enlist as a Drummer Boy. No, came the reply, they weren't taking those either. I formed the impression that they did not want me at all, and so after a while applied to the Scots Guards.

The following jottings cover the time from when I enlisted until I went to the Royal Armoured Corps Officer Cadet Training Unit at Sandhurst. As for many others, my time as a Guardsman, and especially as a recruit at Caterham, was an experience which I have never forgotten or regretted, tough though that experience was. Drill played a prominent part in our training, and it is hardly surprising that I vividly remember what I call 'The Recruits' Prayer':

> Roll on the day
> When God shall say:
> 'Heaven and Earth
> Close Order, March.'

'SCOTS GUARDS REVERT TO TYPE.
NO ENGLISHMEN NEED APPLY'

In September 1928 a press reporter approached a Recruiting Officer in Whitehall. 'Why,' he asked, 'are you suddenly filling the Scots Guards with Scotsmen?'

The Recruiting Officer looked surprised. 'Why not?' he replied. 'Orders, that's all. Irishmen for the Irish Guards, Welshmen for the Welsh Guards, now Scotsmen for the Scots Guards. Natural enough, surely.'

It was suggested that if it was as normal as all that, there was no need to issue a Special Order. The Recruiting Officer seemed shocked.

'You can't have an Army without Orders,' he said. 'We have orders every day. Orders and orders and orders. Look at these.' He produced a massive file and thumbed its contents affectionately. 'Orders, every one of them,' he said angrily. 'What's unusual about that? You must have orders, y'know.'

'How do you tell the difference between a Scotsman, an Irishman and Welshman?' he was asked.

'By their parents,' he glared. 'If you were born in Malta, you wouldn't be Maltese, would you?'

'Are there many Scotsmen in the Scots Guards now?' he was asked.

'Lots of them,' he said, 'but I won't tell you how many.' That, apparently, is an Army Secret.

RECRUITING TALES

These anecdotes relate to many years later, but are recorded here because of the subject.

The Scots Guards sent a contingent to raise recruits in

"What do you mean — I look like something out of Carnaby Street? I AM something out of Carnaby Street."
Cartoon by Giles. *By permission of Express Newspapers*

Perthshire. Our activities ranged from appearing at the Pitlochry Games to tug of war at the Braemar Gathering. At the former I left an indelible mark on the memories of some who were present, and who may read these jottings, by saying over the loudspeaker system, 'Good people of Pitlochry, we salute you, and you in your turn should return our Salutation.' I then paused for the expected response, but was met by a deadly silence. There are some Scots who are a little undemonstrative. At Braemar we won the Tug of War, and I was invited back to the nearby castle, which I hasten to add was *not* Balmoral. I was somewhat alarmed when my hostess remarked, 'Come into my boudoir, you Gorgeous Beast!'

A singular occasion was a visit to a small town through which ran an extremely long street. I was invited by the Provost to his house at 11 a.m. for a 'planning conference' at which the whisky consumption was higher on the agenda than the planning. At any rate, in the event, we got off on time, marching down this street until we saw the Provost and his party assembled on a platform on the pavement. At this point we halted and it was my opportunity to spread my message. (It would be an exaggeration to say that hysteria was sweeping through the populace at our appearance and march. The pavements were somewhat lightly thronged.)

'Provost,' I said, 'never in the whole history of the Scots Guards, going back to when we were raised in 1642, has there been a time when a man from your town has not been in our ranks.' (This was, on reflection, improbable and certainly untrue at the time I spoke those words.) And I continued for a while in the same vein. When I finished, the Provost pressed a switch on his microphone. There was a blinding flash, and he and his entourage were enveloped in green smoke. He was left speechless, so we moved to the right in threes and carried on our way. I often wonder if there is yet a man from this town in our ranks.

ENLISTMENT

When I went to the Recruiting Office in New Scotland Yard, the occasion was one that was never to be forgotten.

It so happened that there were in the queue ahead of me two young men who were also joining up. The Sergeant was taking down the particulars and said to the first:

'Right, lad, don't be nervous. Name?'

And he replied, 'Lord _____ .'

'Good God,' commented the Sergeant. 'Just shows we 'ave to take in all sorts now,' and completed the form. 'Next,' he said. 'Name?'

'The Earl of _____ .'

'Now, now, boy, don't you try to be funny.' But it was the truth: he was an Earl.

When it came to the third in the line—me—who happened to be a Commoner, the Sergeant said, 'Don't tell me: you must be Jesus Christ.'

After the medical test came the intelligence test. The first question was simple: two circles and a square; what was the odd one? But it became progressively more difficult.

When I had completed it, I handed it to the Sergeant and sat down. A few minutes later the Sergeant returned, peered at me suspiciously, asked who I was and if I was feeling all right, and withdrew. A Warrant Officer appeared and did the same, and then I was ushered in to the Recruiting Office.

'You've put down here that you want to join the Scots Guards,' he said.

'Yes, sir.'

'Well, you can't do that.'

'Why not, sir, aren't I good enough?'

'You'd better sit down,' the officer said. 'Now, my job is to put the round pegs into the round holes. Do you realise that this intelligence test was designed by very clever professors, and *you* have not only completed it without a single mistake, but in half the time that was thought possible? You can't possibly go into the Scots Guards.'

Goodness knows what the officer had in mind for me: I might have been appointed Churchill's right hand man. Being an honest boy, however, I disclosed that not only had I done the test three times before but had had it corrected. The Recruiting Officer was *not* amused—but I got into the Scots Guards!

ANY COMPLAINTS?

Naturally recruits marched to meals, eaten off tables which had been scrubbed white. The ration of tea per table was the contents of a highly polished bucket (and it tasted like it). Before the repast was over, the room was called to Attention, at which command we all sat bolt upright. 'Any complaints?' asked the Picquet Officer, to which the response was to be, 'No, sir,' in unison.

On one occasion, however, the unheard of *was* heard. A recruit daringly piped up, 'Yes, sir.' It was reminiscent of the famous H.M. Bateman cartoon, 'The Guardsman who dropped his rifle'! The Company Quartermaster Sergeant, Master Cook and sundry other NCOs escorted the officer to where the miscreant sat.

'Did I hear you correctly?' he was asked.

'Yes, sir. The porridge is burnt.'

'Burnt!' exclaimed the Entourage.

'I say,' remarked the officer.

'Yes, sir'—and 400 other recruits would have agreed with him.

The Picquet Officer was offered a spoon and hesitantly he took a small sample. 'Delicious,' he declared. 'Take his name. Don't you know there's a war on?'

The recruit not only lost his name but was removed from sight, while we all thought he deserved the VC. I cannot recall any repeat of such an act of bravery during my time at the Guards Depot.

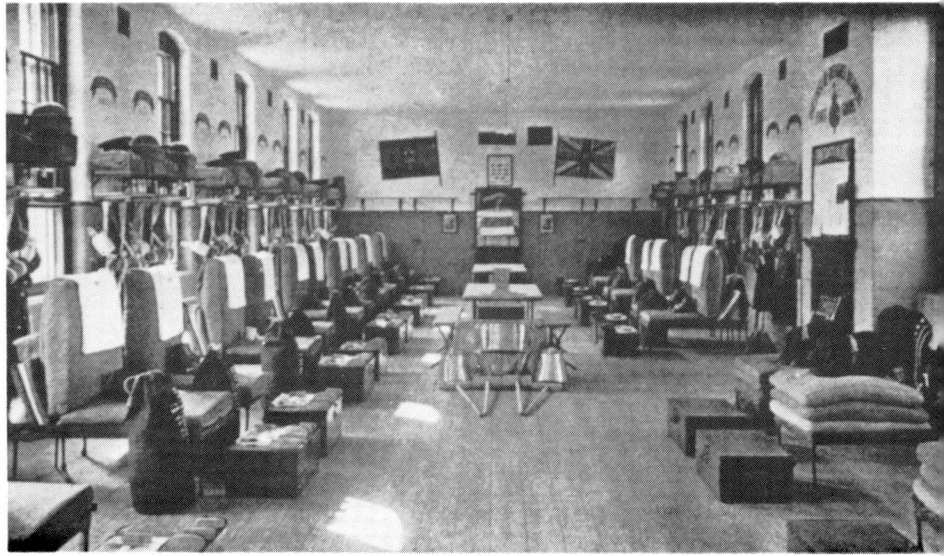

A Barrack Room, 1935. In 1942 the Guards Depot was expanded and a large hutted camp constructed around the Fox Inn (which still stands). Although recruits were accommodated in barrack huts, the interiors had changed little since 1935, except that the beds were three planks on two low trestles. The same perfection in kit layout was expected—and achieved—or else!

A FULL KIT INSPECTION

Everything had to be perfect, and to achieve perfection took time. As a result, recruits slept on the floor, leaving their kit laid out on the beds.

Next morning each recruit stood by his bed, chanting to the Inspecting Officer his number, rank and name, adding, 'Washing at the wash, otherwise kit present and ready for your inspection, *sir*.'

The Officer gazed at one recruit's layout and, picking up a pair of socks on the end of his walking stick, said, 'Trained Soldier, these socks are disgusting. Take his name.' They were new, unworn and kept only for inspection. Such was life.

THE DEPOT SERGEANT MAJOR

The smartest man I ever saw was called Dunn. He was in the Welsh Guards and, in 1942, the Regimental Sergeant Major of the Guards Depot, Caterham.

One very hot morning he appeared on the barrack square, and

"Sergeant! Look at all this hair!"
Cartoon by Osbert Lancaster, from *Signs of the Times. Reproduced by permission of The Estate of Sir Osbert Lancaster and John Murray (Publishers) Ltd*

it was as if God had arrived. He was immaculate and he said to our Squad instructor, 'I'll take over now, Sergeant,' then he turned and spoke as follows:

'Pay attention to me, you scruffy, idle recruits. You are very privileged indeed to be serving the King in His Majesty's Brigade of Guards. You have been issued with this expensive uniform'— (it was only battle dress, but never mind)—'and equipped with these precision, hand-made rifles. They are so perfectly balanced, they'll stand up by themselves.'

Had I enjoyed a scientific rather than a classical education, I might have known better, but God had spoken and it *must* be true. We were standing 'easy' and I took my hand away. Down crashed the rifle, and I was in the guardroom in very quick time!

THE GRENADIER CUSTOM

'Now,' said the Grenadier Guards Company Sergeant Major, 'when in a minute you are marched before the Company Commander at what *we* call 'Company Memorandum', I don't care what regiment you are in. You will comply with *our* customs. If you are asked a question you are first to say, "I thank you, sir, for leave to speak".' And, turning to (and on) a Scots Guards recruit, 'Do you understand?'

'Yes, sir.'

'Don't say, "Yes, sir". Say, "Sir".'

'But I have, sir,' said the Jock.

'You are a hopeless, idle man. Stop talking and fall in!'

When at last I stood before the Company Commander, having rehearsed continuously in my mind the correct phrase, I was asked if I had anything to say. 'I leave you, sir, with thanks to speak.' And leave I did in very quick time and never said another word.

LEAVING THE DEPOT

The recruits, on leaving the Depot for the Guards Armoured Training Wing, were marched in one by one before the Commandant—a World War I veteran with one eye, a peer of the realm and a Coldstreamer.

'You have done surprisingly well,' he said to me. 'Take your Latrines, for example. I've never seen anything so good in all my life. If you continue as you have begun, I think there is a promising career ahead of you. March out.'

He was right: my 'swabbing task' was a block of latrines. I had sandpapered the seats, burnished the chains, and hung a sign, 'Out of Order', at the entrance, which I only removed for inspections. I rose to be a full General commanding an Army Group.

IMPROPERLY DRESSED

There was once a drill movement which was taught and frequently practised at the Guards Depot and in Training Battalions during the war: how to salute when improperly dressed. It could be done to the left, to the right and, combined with a halt and subsequent about turn, to the front. The three middle fingers were placed on the top of the cap which was then removed to the side of the body for the correct length of time before being replaced and the right arm cut away.

On the last day before being posted from Pirbright to the Royal Armoured Corps Officer Cadet Training Unit at Sandhurst, I was determined to salute in this fashion 'for real'. Accordingly I left the barrack hut wearing a smart Service Dress cap with a stitched peak, shirt, braces, denims and boots. I was looking for an officer and, passing the YMCA, saw one walking towards me from the Mess. This was the moment! I carried out the drill

67

Army Form B2091.

RECRUIT'S DEPOT TRAINING REPORT (Infantry).

.... DEPOT........ GUARDS

Army No ....2701193....
Rank ....Gdsn.Rct.....
Name ....Gow, James Michael....
Date of Enlistment....7.8.42.
  ,, Birth....3.6.24
Religion ....C/E....
Trade on Enlistment ....Student....

Terms of Service—Colours 4
                Reserve 8
Previous Service (if any) .... ----

No. of weeks training 8
Days lost—Sick....Nil....Absent....Nil
Posted to Bn....21 OCTU - 10.10.42.

WEAPON TRAINING PROFICIENCY.

    (a) Rifle *Very good. Keen & workmanlike* (b) L.M.G. *V.good.*

        Score *65*

        Classification *1st*

        REMARKS (*e.g.*, No. of rounds fired at (i) 30-yds., or (ii) "open" ranges). *RIFLE 20 L.M.G. 2*

FIELD CRAFT PROFICIENCY.

DRILL PROFICIENCY.
Excellent

PHYSICAL TRAINING EFFICIENCY. *Manifested a high degree of efficiency. Worked really hard.*

    Field Tests........ Standard Tests........No. of periods required to complete........

    Weight (a) on enlistment........ *150 lbs.*........ (b) At the end of training........ *162 lbs.*

ANTI-GAS.

EDUCATION.—Grade on enlistment........ Certificate obtained........

SPORTS.

INTELLIGENCE AND CHARACTER.
Both very good

KEENNESS AND CLEANLINESS.
Very keen and clean.

REMARKS BY O.C. TRAINING COY.* *RECRUIT LEADER who should prove an excellent leader as a Coy. Officer. Has done extremely well*

* If the Recruit has held the appointment of Acting Lance-Corporal the fact should be stated.

Station........

Date........ *30 SEP 1942*

Forms/B2091/32

        Henry Archer Pilkington
              LT. COLONEL
        OFFICER COMMANDING GUARDS DEPOT

Commanding Depot........

H.S. Goodhart-Rendel Captain.
Comdg. 14th Coy

movement, much to the officer's surprise, but the incident was marred when a voice shouted, 'Come 'ere, lad.' It was a Drill Sergeant who placed me under close arrest—for being improperly dressed.

4

Days as a Young Officer

I was commissioned as a 2nd Lieutenant (or Ensign) into the Scots Guards in 1943, and the following random jottings cover a period up to the time I passed the entrance examination and was selected to attend the course at the Army Staff College, Camberley in 1954. I was lucky enough to be posted to the 3rd (Tank) Battalion Scots Guards, the officers of which were subsequently to achieve a pretty impressive and unique record:

THE FOLLOWING OFFICERS SERVED IN THE THIRD (TANK) BATTALION
SCOTS GUARDS

The Archbishop of Canterbury
The Lord Chamberlain
The Home Secretary (later Lord President of the Council, and leader of the House of Commons and House of Lords)
The Marshal of the Diplomatic Corps and Colonel The Life Guards
The Chairman of United Biscuits
The Chairman of Scottish and Newcastle Breweries
The Chairman of Rolls-Royce
The Chairman of the Baltic Exchange
The Moderator of the General Assembly of the Church of Scotland
The Commodore of the Royal Yacht Squadron
The Headmaster of Marylebone Grammar School

Lieutenant Robert Runcie (later the Archbishop of Canterbury) in Paris, 1944. *Photo David Bankes collection*

Major W. S. I. Whitelaw, the 2nd in Command, at Siebeneichen, Germany, May 1945, later Viscount Whitelaw of Penrith, Lord President of the Council and Leader of the House of Lords. "I took on this challenge that if Hitler was announced dead, which I didn't think he would be, I would immediately smoke a large cigar. I was woken up at 7.30 a.m. on 1 May, a week before VE Day, by a friend, who brought in the cigar with the news that his death had been announced and that I had to smoke it straight away. I went down to breakfast smoking this thing and to the fury of my friends it didn't do me any harm at all. Then on VE Day I smoked my second cigar and I have never smoked another one since." *Photo David Bankes collection*

71

The Chief Scout of the Commonwealth
The President of the Boys' Brigade
The Senior Steward of the Jockey Club
The President of the Royal British Legion, Scotland

The Battalion produced:

1 General
2 Lieutenant Generals
4 Major Generals
4 Lords Lieutenant
2 Knights of the Thistle
2 Lords High Commissioner of the General Assembly of the
  Church of Scotland
1 Ambassador
1 Commander-in-Chief British Army of the Rhine
1 General Officer Commanding Northern Ireland
3 General Officers Commanding Berlin
2 Major Generals Commanding Household Division
2 Governors of Edinburgh Castle
2 Colonels Commandant of the Scottish Division of Infantry.

TWO REMARKABLE SCOTS GUARDS OFFICERS

From an outstanding collection of officers to be found in the 3rd (Tank) Battalion Scots Guards, I take but two:

Harold Llewellyn Smith's father had been Permanent Secretary to the Board of Trade and Economic Adviser to the Government. Harold was an exhibitioner at Winchester College, a Scholar of New College Oxford, where he was the Stanhope Prize winner, and he devoted his life to teaching and boys' clubs. In 1940 he joined the 'Local Defence Volunteers', later known as the Home Guard, and his Group Commander reported that he was 'the best officer of his rank in the West of Cornwall HG—11,000 strong'. Aged 36, he enlisted as a Guardsman in the Scots Guards and on commissioning became the battalion Signals Officer. Here was an officer much older than his contemporaries and the ex-senior history master of Marylebone Grammar School. He was immensely erudite, a little forbidding but with a delightful sense of humour. The breadth of his knowledge was so singular that I was determined to ask him something to which he could not possibly know the answer. We were in an orchard in the Normandy bridgehead in 1944. 'Harold,' I said, what do you know of the Constitution of the State of Andorra?' He removed his pipe from his mouth, turned a lugubrious gaze upon me and replied, 'Everything. My father wrote a book about it!'

The battalion chaplain, later to become the Moderator of the General Assembly of the Church of Scotland, was dearly loved by all ranks. The officers occasionally pulled his leg, as when he preached a sermon in which he mentioned 'the slippery pit of sexual excess'. This was such an instant success that he was badgered to give more than one repeat performance, supported by a popular hymn, 'Yield not to temptation, bad language disdain . . .'

73

One day, again in Normandy, he and I sought permission to visit Deauville, which had fairly recently been liberated. I drove the jeep and the Rev. George Reid read the map. We got to our destination but George found it impossible to find the way back. Our every turn was stopped by signs saying, 'ACHTUNG! MINEN!' Time passed and we began to feel hungry. 'This is a crisis,' said George. 'We must open the emergency rations or we shall starve,' and this we did. George then remarked that he was feeling rather tired and found in the emergency pack some potent looking pep-up tablets which, so it said on the label, were guaranteed to keep one awake and alert. George ate two (just to make sure), returned to his map and within three minutes was fast asleep. How we got back was a miracle!

THE INTERVIEW

Two newly commissioned officers were instructed to report to the Regimental Adjutant before joining the Training Battalion. This was wartime, but nevertheless they were told that they must not carry parcels in the street or travel by public transport, and in general were given the sort of guidance which must have been relevant in the 1920s. On departure, therefore, it was with some surprise that they saw the Lieutenant Colonel Commanding the Regiment departing for luncheon in the Guards Club on a bicycle. He was, moreover, wearing an Army Gas Cape.

THE COURT MARTIAL

Three young officers were ordered to attend a Court Martial under instruction. The Accused was asked by the President if he had any objections to him and to the other officers who were members of the Court. 'No, sir,' came the reply, 'but what I do object to is that row of bloody sparrers sitting there!'

PIPE TUNES

On 28 March, 1944, the Adjutant of the 3rd Tank Battalion Scots Guards issued a letter to all officers. 'The standard of knowledge of the names of pipe tunes among the officers of this Battalion is depressingly low. The following list is therefore circulated so that officers, having learnt them, may appear better educated in this

Advice to young officers: if asked in almost any possible situation by a senior officer what you would do, it is safe to reply, "Inspect the men's feet." Officers are expected to set an example in foot hygiene, as illustrated by Major Sir Charles Maclean in Normandy, 1944. (Later the Lord Maclean, Lord Chamberlain.) *Photo David Bankes collection*

matter.' And there followed the names of 39 Marches, 12 Strathspeys and reels ('as they go together'), seven Slow Marches and six Retreats.

The following day a letter headed, 'Subject: Waterproofing and all that', was issued over the signature of the Technical Adjutant to 'Squadron Leaders and other small fry': 'The standard of knowledge of technical phraseology among the officers of the Battalion is gloriously low. The following list will be learnt forthwith so that officers may be waterproofed at the shortest notice. You are no good tactically if you cannot float.'

The list was captioned 'Track Spares and Wheels (as they go together)', and a few items are as follows:

Petrol and Jerrican Gathering   Ferry Bus
Loose Bonnets   Mary Bang the Lever
My road to sprint on   Muckin' of gorgeous tyres
Lock of the Torque   Towed to the Isles
Wheel in the kitchen   Wheel among the Trailers
The Highland Cradle's wrong   The Rejected Tooter
Froze among the Heather   Bother the Brig!
The Green Pills of Cyril*   Rattle of the Boot

*Captain Cyril Cunningham, Scots Guards

ROUGH JUSTICE

The Battalion finished the war in Schleswig Holstein. The Commanding Officer appointed the 2nd in Command, who eventually became the Deputy Prime Minister, as the local Military Governor. The latter issued an order that all Nazi Party officials were to be arrested and brought before him.

I was despatched to apprehend the local Ortsgruppenleiter, which I was determined to do in style. I pictured myself stopping my jeep at the door with squealing brakes, followed by a half track with siren going. Things didn't quite work out as planned: the brakes did not squeal, the siren failed and I stopped at the wrong house. However, the Ortsgruppenleiter conveniently emerged from next door and climbed aboard the half track, carrying his night case.

Next morning he was 'marched in' by one Sgt Angus, an ex-AA patrolman from the Highlands, before the 2nd in Command. The evidence was delivered by some French Prisoners of War in French which was translated (by a Scots Guards officer) inaccurately into German. The accused had nothing to say—no doubt because he had no idea what he was being asked.

Most impressively, the 2nd in Command scowled and said (in English) 'You are guilty. I order you to be removed, to a place to which, no doubt, in the past, you have yourself committed so many others. Take him away, Sgt Angus.' And removed he was, by the scruff of the neck.

I could not fail to be impressed by the occasion, which indeed left an indelible mark on my mind. And yet, I wondered whether there had not been, perhaps, a miscarriage of justice, and this worried me. (After all, what had we been fighting the war about?)

Next day, however, my conscience was cleared. As I drove through the village, who should I see working in his garden, wearing a straw hat, but the accused Ortsgruppenleiter.

FAREWELL TO ARMOUR PARADE

Guards Armoured Division, joined by 6th Guards Tank Brigade —1,200 infantry and over 200 tanks—assembled on Rotenberg Airfield in Germany on 9 June, 1945, in a 'Farewell to Armour' parade. The *News Guardian*, journal of the Division, reported (*inter alia*):

The sun was shining when the Commander-in-Chief[1] arrived—six minutes late . . . Everyone was there. The Army Commander, General Dempsey,[2] the Major General, two Corps Commanders, several Divisional Commanders, and so many other Brass Hats that Brigadiers were ten a penny. The Navy and RAF were there in force. There were even some of the *Wehrmacht* who had been marched up from their prison camp . . . If all the loud-speakers had been working, the audience might have heard the Field Marshal. As it was many did not hear a word.

The following vignettes were reported:

Overheard in the Enclosure: 'Don't fancy tabbing it—nowhere to carry the loot.' 'Marlene Dietrich was born in Rotenberg.' 'Someone ought to put him in the book—six minutes late!' 'Eight thousand gallons of paint were used—Scots Guards spent $14\frac{1}{2}$ minutes obtaining their final correct dressing before the C-in-C arrived—casualties, mechanical: all tanks left the field under their own power; two broke down shortly afterwards—doubtless due to nervous exhaustion.'

THE TALE OF THE TRANSFEREE

In 1948 Home Service Clothing (or Full Dress) was restored to the Foot Guards on the Public Duties. The Colour of the 2nd Battalion Scots Guards was to be trooped on the King's Birthday Parade, and photographs were taken of the various Guards, furnished by that Battalion, when they were practising on the square at Chelsea Barracks.

It was customary for staff officers of the Regiment, if they so wished, to lunch in the Mess at Chelsea. One day, when a Company Commander was looking at these photographs, he was joined by an officer from Headquarters London District, who

---

[1] Field Marshal Montgomery.
[2] Commanding 2nd Army.

It's difficult to recognise someone under a bearskin . . .

kept asking, 'Who's that? Who's that? I can't recognise these officers under their bearskins.' Eventually, slightly exasperated and wanting to go in to lunch, the Company Commander said, 'Well, you wouldn't know *him* anyhow. He transferred in from "outside" three weeks ago.'

The Staff Officer was staggered, so much so that he had to order another drink.

'Transferred in? Where from? No one told me. It really is too bad of Regimental Headquarters. What's his name?'

'Knatchbull-Ferguson.'

'Well, what's his seniority, I wonder—has he slipped in over me?'

'I've no idea,' came the reply. 'You'd better ask him yourself.'

Day after day the Staff Officer haunted the Mess, in search of K-F, but he was never there. He was either away on duty, on a course, on leave or—oh, horror!—Captain of the King's Guard.

His letter rack was invariably bulging with mail, which the Staff Officer examined—and reported to his friends as apparently coming either from sleazy night clubs, dubious bookies or from postmarks he had never heard of ('Where's Tooting?').

The stories related about him and his behaviour horrified the Staff Officer: he overheard the Commander of Headquarters Company say to the Adjutant, '*Someone* must tell this chap the form. Probably not his fault, but do you know what he said yesterday? "I'll just check up with the CO about one of my lads being Orderly Dog next week. Okey Dokey?".'

His misdemeanours, the question of his seniority, his lack of appearance—all these practically gave the Staff Officer a heart attack. He suggested to the Second-in-Command that, much as he flinched from the task, *he* would be prepared to have a word with K-F if it would help. After all, the honour of the Battalion—nay, of the Regiment—was at stake (What would the Grenadiers think if it leaked out?).

The short answer as to why he could not was because K-F did not exist and never had.

. . . until he takes it off. "Caps off . . . Three cheers for Her Majesty The Queen!" Holyroodhouse, Edinburgh. *Photo George Outram & Co Ltd*

WARTIME QUALITY

'You know,' said a male guest to the Captain of the Queen's Guard during luncheon at St James's Palace, 'we took some very odd people into the Regiment during the War.'

'As Guardsmen?'

'No, No. As Officers.'

'Well, I can't recall anyone all that peculiar. Who do you mean?'

'I'll tell you,' said the guest, 'though I don't like thinking about it even now. I remember going into the Mess one day. It was before lunch. There was a young chap sitting there, he'd only been commissioned two days. What do you think he was doing?'

'I've no idea.'

'He was reading—a book! I went up behind him to see what it was. And what do you think it was?'

'Pornography.'

'No, *far* worse, Shakespeare! I knew at once he was no good.'

MRS SMITH

The 2nd Battalion Scots Guards was sent to the Far East for what was known as 'the Malayan Emergency', and carried out anti-terrorist operations from 1948 to 1951. Operations consisted of patrols, ambushes and raids, and for most who took part the lasting memory is one's first patrol into the jungle. The Battalion comprised many conscripted men doing their period of National Military Service, and on one such patrol, while the Company was preparing a temporary camp, deep in the jungle, the Company Commander asked a newcomer what he thought of it. The Guardsman considered for a while and gave the memorable, whispered reply: 'Mrs Smith wouldna feel at hame here, sir!'

The officers of the Queen's Guard in the Guardroom at St James's Palace.

83

Pahang, Malaya. This is where Mrs Smith would *not* have felt at home . . .

. . . But this is a bit like Auchterarder, perhaps.

A VISIT TO THAILAND?

Two Thai Officers were attached to a Scots Guards battalion while stationed in Singapore for a period of rest and recuperation from duties in the Malayan Emergency.

At the last dinner in the Mess before returning to the fray, a Company Commander said to one of them, 'Do you know, I've never been to your country. Do you think I should?'

'Oh yes, certainly,' he replied. 'Plenty to do.'

'Oh good—shooting, fishing?'

'Yes, Yes.'

'Nice places to see? Swimming on sandy beaches?'

'Oh yes, yes.'

'It sounds splendid, I'd love to.'

'Yes, yes—naturally—and love, too!'

A HUSBAND'S REACTION

I once commanded the 'Brigade Squad', composed of potential officers for the Household Cavalry and Foot Guards, on a highly concentrated and tough course at Caterham. For some offences I

Selarang Barracks, Singapore, 1 January, 1950. The Regimental History records: "On the 3 January 1950 the Battalion left for the north; only the proximity of Hogmanay can explain the arrival at the destination of certain parts of the Main Body *before* the Advance Party." Above are three members of that very party.

awarded 'Extra Fatigues', which could be carried out in the garden of my Quarter.

The crime rate seemed to be increasing, and one afternoon I went to the house and peered through the hedge to see how the defaulters were getting on with their 'fatigues'. To my amazement, there they were lying on rugs on the lawn, reading magazines—and through the french windows came my wife with a jug of tea and 'wads' (alias buns). 'Are any of you going to the Queen Charlotte's Ball this evening?' she charmingly asked!

A WIFELY REACTION

I came home for lunch. I lived with my family in a Quarter in the middle of the Guards Depot at Caterham, and was met by my wife, clearly in a state of upset: 'I've seen something awful today. It was on the barrack square.'

'Not an instructor striking a recruit?'

'Far worse,' she replied. 'You would hardly believe it possible. When the boys were being drilled, some of their hats fell off—and the Sergeant never even picked them up!'

A ROYAL GAME OF CARDS

As a newly appointed Equerry, I was paying my first visit to Barnwell, the country home of the late Duke of Gloucester and Princess Alice. As I went up to my room to change for dinner, the Lady-in-Waiting murmured, 'Don't forget, Canasta after dinner.'

'Canasta,' I replied, 'what's that?'

'My goodness,' she said, 'you *have* been badly briefed.' The book of rules was hastily produced, but time was pressing, and the faster I read, the less I understood the rules.

After the dinner the table was set up and His Royal Highness paired with me against the Duchess and the Lady-in-Waiting. Thanks to my ineptitude, we lost by more points than had ever been thought possible. Not only was the result regrettable but the scene was somewhat bizarre as the Duke wore his Scots Guards bearskin cap throughout the game (to ensure a good fit for the forthcoming Trooping).

'Next time,' remarked Her Royal Highness, 'I think we'd better play Scrabble!'

ROYAL MINUTES

His late Royal Highness Prince Henry, Duke of Gloucester, was the Senior Colonel of what is now called the Household Division. As well as being his Equerry I was also the Assistant Regimental Adjutant, so he told me to convene a meeting of the Colonels at York House. Afterwards I produced minutes which I showed to the Duke.

'These are no use. All wrong. Leave it to me.' And with what looked like a carpenter's pencil, the minutes were altered beyond recognition and sent back to me with instructions to despatch them to the Major General.

Two days later I was telephoned by the ADC and told that the Major General was coming on the line.

'Those minutes are dreadful; I can't understand a word. *If* you wrote them you should be sacked.'

'No, sir, it was not I. It was the Duke of Gloucester.' End of conversation.

THE EDUCATION OF A YOUNG OFFICER

I was appointed Quartermaster of a District Cadet Camp, and when the cadets had left the Acting Quartermaster Sergeant said, 'Slight difficulty here, sir.'

'Oh really?'

'Deficient of 92 sheets.'

'Oh, what happens?'

'Well, *you* pay.'

I was aghast. 'Pay? But I've got a wife and two children! I can't pay. You *must* help me.'

'Now don't worry,' came the reply, 'tomorrow we'll have the sheets back. You watch carefully and you'll learn a useful lesson.'

Next day the sheets were handed back to the Barrack Officer in a small hut, divided down the middle by racking. As 'Barracks' counted the sheets through his legs, they were picked up, passed round and counted again—so that the Quartermaster ended up with a surplus.

Afterwards I said to the Acting Quartermaster Sergeant, 'You can't do that. It's downright immoral.' 'Come, come, sir,' came the reply. 'If you take that view you'll never get anywhere in the Army.'

A SUDDEN CALL TO DUTY

I was the Acting Quartermaster at Pirbright. One summer evening I was at home in a tiny mews house in London when the telephone rang. It was the Commanding Officer:

'The Major General has told me that the Commander of Number 4 Guard on the Trooping is not up to scratch and must not appear on parade. *You* will take his place.'

'But, sir, the Trooping is the day after tomorrow. I've done none of the rehearsals.'

'Never mind that,' came the reply. 'You did it some time back and you will just have to mug it up.'

'But what about my tunic, sword. . . ?'

'You'd better go down first thing tomorrow to the Regimental Stores and get kitted out.'

'As I'm really the Quartermaster, I suppose I should wear a cocked hat rather than a bearskin?' There was a pause and back came the Commanding Officer.

'Don't be a bloody fool. Of course not. I always thought you quite intelligent!' And that was that.

Came Saturday and 'the Day'. How I got through, only God—and the Company Sergeant Major who was in earshot—knew. A running commentary from the Ensign of the Guard—a Scottish Peer—saved the day!

THE RUMOUR

The day before a State Visit began, before lunch in the Officers' Mess at Wellington Barracks, I facetiously remarked over a drink, 'Wouldn't it be funny if, as the President of Italy got into the carriage with the Queen at Victoria Station to drive to the Palace, the Crown Equerry handed him a note which read "*Non Sputare della carrozza.*" This was greeted with a titter at the speaker's inanity.

Two days later I heard a member in the Guards Club say to another, 'Do you know what happened yesterday at Victoria? I wouldn't have believed it if I hadn't actually seen it with my own eyes. The Crown Equerry stepped forward and . . .'

The passage of rumour is indeed rapid.

SWORD DRILL

In the Foot Guards only a Regimental Sergeant Major, amongst the Warrant Officers, draws his sword on parade, and that on one occasion: the parade which marks the Sovereign's Birthday. There was, however, one instance when this custom was broken by a Drill Sergeant, and the circumstances were as follows:

Some years ago the 2nd Battalion Scots Guards furnished a Guard of Honour with the State Colour for the arrival by the Queen in the Royal Train at the now defunct Caledonian Station, Edinburgh. After Her Majesty had been greeted with a Royal Salute and had inspected her Foot Guards, she and her Household left by car for the Palace of Holyroodhouse.

The Guard of Honour then marched out of the Station behind the Regimental Band, but a few seconds after they had started off down the platform, a drama ensued as is evidenced in the following conversation:

Drill Sergeant, hurrying up to the Guard Commander on the line of march: 'For God's sake, sir, step short!'
Commander: 'Don't be stupid. If I do that, we'll lose the band.'
Drill Sergeant: 'You must, sir, the top of the Colour pole's caught up in the British Rail bunting, and the Ensign looks as if he is playing a Salmon.'
Commander: 'Well, *do* something, Drill Sergeant, and get a move on.'

The Drill Sergeant saluted, drew his sword, slashed the bunting, and the State Colour, the Honour of the Regiment (and the Guard of Honour) were saved. Thus is history made!

Caledonian Station, Edinburgh. The Inspection before the Sword Slash.
Photo The Scotsman Publications Ltd

5
The Army Staff College

Entry to the Staff College for the one year course was, and still is, considered to be one of the most important 'hurdles' in an officer's career. Indeed many think that if an officer fails to get to Camberley, his prospects are bleak indeed.

I was lucky enough to scrape through the written exam which lasted five days, and to attend the course. I was even luckier to be selected later to return to Camberley as one of the Instructors on the Directing Staff, where the work load was *far* harder.

There follow a few memories of both these periods to which I have added an anecdote called 'the Burgermeister's Reception', not because it has anything to do with Camberley, but it occurred after I left as a student for my first staff appointment as Brigade Major in Germany. It does not conveniently fit in elsewhere!

COMMENTS OF THE STAFF COLLEGE INSTRUCTIONAL STAFF

At Camberley the written work of the students is always read, corrected and commented upon by a member of the Directing Staff (DS) in red ink. Some of these comments are the cause of grave concern to the student, who wonders whether his performance is so indifferent that he may be sacked. They were (and doubtless still are), however, sources of amusement and delight to the DS who thinks them up. It is said that when he was one of these, Monty (Field Marshal Viscount Montgomery of Alamein) wrote on the work of some luckless student: 'A *very* marked improvement; thoroughly bad work!'

Sometimes the Commandant sees samples of the work upon which he comments in green ink. On one occasion the students were instructed to produce a long, historical thesis; one subject was 'Compare the Russo-Japanese, Boer, and Great Wars. . .' A particular student appreciated that his effort would be improved by footnotes, producing a more impressive and erudite layout. Thus, for example, he would write. ' "A greater weight of shell fell upon the defenders during the siege of Mukden than on any previous recorded occasion." Footnote: Toumai Takarai, *Russo-Japanese War*. Vol. 1, page 98. Oxford University Press, 1913.' And there were many others of that ilk supporting his thesis.

The DS passed the paper up the line till it arrived with the Commandant who sent it back with this comment. 'First class work. You must have spent a lot of time in research. Keep it up!'

The student did keep it up, but in this case not much effort was involved. He had invented them all.

MILITARY ADVICE

'It is vital to read the question with care, and then answer it,' exhorted the Instructor. The students were issued with the paper. 'Do you think the guided missile is the future "Queen of the Battlefield?" Do not write more than 5,000 words.'

The students set to work; some even visited the library for research. One, however, wrote his name, initials, rank and number on the top of a blank sheet, added the title of the subject, wrote 'No', handed it in and went home. He had read and answered the question.

THE METHOD SYSTEM IN ACTING

A senior member of the Directing Staff addressed the students before a 'Telephone Battle'. "In a moment I will give you envelopes, inside which you will find notes telling you of your appointment in this important exercise. When you know what you are, play your part fully. For example, if you are the Chief Clerk, think of your career in the RAOC—your wife in your

A 'Tactical Exercise without Troops'. Staff College, Camberley. The Directing Staff waits for the students to decide what to do. The 'correct' solution, naturally, is that of the senior officer present.

Sometimes this produces a droll solution. A General visited training and was incensed by the shambles he witnessed. Furious, he exclaimed, "I've never seen anything so inefficient in my life. Who is the senior officer here?" To which the reply, quite accurately, was, "You, sir!"

94

Warrant Officer's Quarter, life in the Sergeants' Mess and so on. It's called the Method System.'

One student, a distinguished Coldstreamer, found that he was the Divisional Commander and, remembering his Instructor's directions, dressed up with red tabs as a Major General. He set up his headquarters in a lecture hall and surrounded by his staff, was pacing up and down, thinking what a General should be thinking, when in came the Commandant. At once the student went up and slapped him on the back. 'Hullo, Dudley, haven't seen you for ages.'

This was not well received.

A STAFF COLLEGE VIGNETTE

The Commandant convened a 'Think Session', attended not only by all members of the Directing Staff but also by a number of distinguished guests, one of whom was the late Sir Basil Liddell Hart. The topics under discussion were wide-ranging and included, for example, 'Is the armoured Hovercraft the Tank of the future?' Ample opportunity was thus afforded to those ambitious DS who hoped to further their careers by showing 'progressive thought'.

'Psst. Can I ask a question?' whispered the French Liaison Officer, who looked like a character from Maigret: crew cut, stocky, petit Caporal permanently stuck to his lip.

'Yes,' replied his friend, 'that's the point of the exercise.'

'No,' said the Frenchman, 'I ask the question of *you*. 'Ave you been to any striptease clubs lately?'

'You can't ask that, for goodness sake. Wait till later.'

'I cannot. I shall forget. I went to one last week. I 'ad only been there five minutes when the patron said, "Ten pounds." "Ten pounds," I replied, "what for?" "Ze wimmin!" Milles Tonnerres! "Wimmin," I said. "They are not wimmin. They are monstairs."'

95

THE COMMITTEE MEETING

I was once detailed to represent the Staff College at an important meeting at which the future acceptance by the Army of a major piece of equipment would be decided. I sat next to a sinister, small man whose eyes were totally obscured by minute, black, steel-rimmed spectacles, and who, I deduced, was from somewhere in the Intelligence community. The important officers and officials addressed each other by the initials of their appointments: 'MGO', 'QMG', 'PUS', 'DMO', 'AUS', etc. etc.[1] The Intelligence man suddenly turned to me and asked, 'Who are you?'

Without thinking, I replied, letter by letter, 'GOW'. 'Oh,' said Dark Eyes, 'that's a new one on me.' It was his sole contribution to the proceedings—and mine!

"A fat lot of use you're going to be dealing with a mechanised breakthrough when it takes you twenty minutes to stop a taxi!" Cartoon by Osbert Lancaster from *Signs of the Times. Reproduced by permission of The Estate of Sir Osbert Lancaster and John Murray (Publishers) Ltd*

[1] Master General of the Ordnance, Quartermaster General, Permanent Under Secretary, Director of Military Operations, Assistant Under Secretary.

A MILITARY QUESTION

Students were constantly told how important it was for Commanders and their staff officers to communicate with subordinates, and particularly with private soldiers.

In the Military District commanded by Major General Wyldbore-Smith was stationed a Battalion which was suddenly ordered to fly to a country which the General knew well. He therefore decided to address All Ranks before they left, to impart some of his experience. He spoke with eloquence and authority, describing the climate, local customs, food and drink, and warning the soldiers of social pitfalls which they might encounter.

When at last he had finished, he said, 'Now I am ready to answer any questions you may have. Don't be shy. Ask *anything*.' Up went a hand. 'Yes?' he asked.

'Please, sir, why have you got such a funny name?'

THE PATENT RANGE SCALE

One of the most imaginative and potentially useful pieces of kit ever invented was the patent range scale. It showed the range of every weapon in the British Army from the two-inch mortar to the heaviest artillery piece. It could be used with maps of two scales and, by placing a pin through one end of the plastic ruler—for that is what it was—marking the weapon's position, it was easy to see how far it could shoot.

I persuaded a firm of military publishers to produce it in quantity and sat back waiting for the royalties to pour in. I even wrote an advert which read, 'An instructor at the Staff College strongly recommends this invaluable "aid" to any staff officer,' which I surreptitiously distributed to students at the start of the next course. (It should be added that the said Instructor was also the inventor.)

97

I could not understand why no money was arriving in my bank account from such a promising source; I knew that *one* had been sold, as a friend had written and underlined his name, adding, 'This line has been drawn with the aid of your patent range scale.'

I visited the Staff College and looked to see if the advert was on the board: it was, but some wag had erased the slogan and substituted, 'A middle-aged Staff Captain (Welfare), Merseyside Sub. District, writes: "I attribute my military success entirely to possessing this range scale"!'

Shortly afterwards the military publishing firm went out of business. They had produced, it was said, 5,000, and sold two.

THE BURGERMEISTER'S RECEPTION

The Garrison Commander, his staff officers and the principal officers of the British units stationed in the German Town were invited to an evening reception in the Town Hall (or *Rathaus*). The date was 1956, the party a little 'sticky': the Germans stood on one side, the British on the other, both holding ever warming glasses of sweet, dark sherry.

After a while the Burgermeister decided to speak. 'This,' he said, 'is the first opportunity that I and the members of the Town Council have had to repay the hospitality of the British.' (Pause.) The Interpreter: 'The Burgermeister says that this is the first time that he and his colleagues have been able to repay the hostility of the British . . .'

The Brigade Major (myself) was so convulsed with the mirth that he had to leave the room, and the following day was reprimanded by the Brigadier for his frivolity.

98

6
Regimental Adjutant

The Household Cavalry and each of the five Regiments of the Foot Guards has a Headquarters: that of the former in the Horse Guards building, Whitehall, and those of the latter in Wellington Barracks. *There* will be found a Major who is called the Regimental Adjutant, an appointment which I filled for three years, much to my delight. The work was varied and interesting. These officers are often involved in ceremonial duties, one of which requires them to be mounted on the Birthday Parade.

THE EQUITATION COURSE

Regimental Adjutants of Foot Guards have to attend an Equitation course run by the Household Cavalry at Knightsbridge Barracks. This is to ensure that they don't fall off during, before or after the Ceremony of Trooping the Colour. I was certainly no natural horseman, but conscientious. My course report from the Riding Master read, 'This officer was the keenest member of the course' (which was gratifying but only meant that I was the only pupil who attended regularly). 'However, his seat is so bad that I can only assume he has some serious physical malformation.'

Paragraph 1005 in Standing Orders of the Household Division reads as follows:

PRECAUTIONS

Horses
Bands and Drums are to play *pianissimo* where necessary to avoid frightening horses.

Although it does not say so specifically, this presumably can only apply to the bands of the Foot Guards, because if the mounted bands of the Household Cavalry complied they would be soundless!

REGIMENTAL PUBLICITY

The Lieutenant Colonel commanding the Scots Guards was always apprehensive about what I, his Regimental Adjutant, was doing or planning to do. This was partly due to his dislike of any

publicity, good or bad. When he asked if I had anything new in mind, I told him:

'I have actually, sir. This year it is the fashion for young ladies to have low-cut backs to their dresses. I am thinking of issuing to all young officers attending dances a rubber stamp so that when their partners are released to leave the floor, imprinted on their backs is the slogan, "Join the Scots Guards. They're a grand bunch".'

The Lieutenant Colonel was speechless.

THE MUSICAL MUSTER

I ordered every single musician, flautist, piper and drummer in the Scots Guards to parade, massed, at the Duke of York's Headquarters in London. The spectacle was unprecedented and impressive, marred only when I noticed a musician lurking on the touch line.

'Now look here,' I said, 'this simply is not good enough. Who are you and why are you not on parade with your instrument?'

'I,' replied the culprit, 'am Musician Goodenough and my instrument is the Grand Piano.'

Case explained.

THE WREATH

I sent for the Superintending Clerk shortly before the Regimental Remembrance Day Parade. 'Last year when we marched to the Guards Memorial to lay the wreath, the old one was still there. It looked inefficient. Send someone to remove it.'

An hour later the Superintending Clerk reported that it had been done, but asked me to look at it. It had lain before the Scots Guards figure at the Memorial for a year, and was indubitably the

Regimental Star, but instead of the motto *Nemo me impune lacessit* was *Quis Separabit*, that of the Irish Guards.

THE CLUB

Many years ago, before the amalgamation with the Cavalry Club took place, the Guards Club in Charles Street was, as usual, in financial straits.

As Regimental Adjutant I was ex-officio a member of the Committee, all of whom otherwise were old and senior.

'This Club will die,' I said at one meeting, 'unless we attract the younger members to use it.' (This was in the days when membership was virtually compulsory for all serving officers.) 'We must move with the times; what *they* want is not necessarily what *you* think they want.'

'What do you propose, then?' I was asked.

'Well, what about turning the basement into a disco and calling it the "Bearskin"?'

The Committee was horrified; one or two looked as if they would have coronaries and I was told to shut up.

'All right, but the least you can do is agree to have a dance for young members,' and with reluctance they agreed.

I applied to the Secretary for ten tickets and was told I could have none—too old! I at once resigned.

7
Commanding Officer
2nd Battalion Scots Guards

To command a battalion of your Regiment is, for an infantry officer, one of the 'peaks' in his career—some go so far as to say that it is *the* peak, that there is nothing before or after which compares, and it is true that the Commanding Officer is Lord of all he surveys. I was fortunate to command a battalion in Kenya and at home. It was during the latter time that we were alerted to be prepared to fly to Rhodesia in the aftermath of Ian Smith's Declaration of Independence. I was summoned to the Ministry of Defence and told to stand by for an unknown destination near Rhodesia, with the leading Company at 24 hours' notice to move. Thus, in this somewhat uncomfortable posture, we remained for several months while we trained *and simultaneously carried out the ceremonial public duties in London*—much to the amazement of a member of the Army Board who could not believe that it was possible! Fortunately, in the event we were never sent.

THE ARRIVAL OF THE NEW COMMANDING OFFICER

I arrived in Kenya to take up my new post, having lost all my kit *en route*, with the exception of a dinner jacket. This did not please the Brigadier who summoned me the following morning with these words:

'You are to stand your battalion to at once, with the leading group at 12 hours' notice to move. You will take a Company of the Staffords[1] under command and be prepared to move by train to Mombasa. There you will embark in a frigate and be ready to make an assault landing by whaler on *that place*. The Brigade Major will answer any questions you may have. Oh, and by the way, I'm off to Aden so you will take over the Brigade as well.' He departed.

'What's "that place" he talks about?' I asked the Brigade Major.

'Zanzibar,' I was told.

'Wherever's that?'

'You haven't been very well briefed, sir. Here it is on the map.'

'But how can I tell where the best places are to assault and who are we assaulting anyhow?'

'Oh don't worry,' came the reply. 'Talk to your Officers' Mess Sergeant. He's a splendid chap and knows the place well.'

Fortunately the operation, which had all the makings of a military fiasco, was never implemented.

---

[1] Another infantry battalion of the same brigade.

THE MILK FLIGHT

I reluctantly left my family in the Mombasa Club and caught the milk flight which left early for Nairobi. A well built, blonde lady sat beside me, and as the plane started down the runway for take off, she said, 'Can I hold your hand or shall I faint?' Once safely airborne the grip was released. 'What do you do?' she asked.

'I'm a soldier,' I replied, and out of politeness enquired, 'And what do *you* do?'

'I'm a stripper.'

I looked at her in some surprise. 'Oh yes, I recognise you. You're "Charming Pilly".'

'That's right,' she said. 'You must have seen my act.'

'No, I'm afraid I haven't, but I recognise you from your picture in the *East African Standard*. You do a turn with "Delectable Delilah".'

'Don't you talk about *her*,' Pilly said, '*she* is a *he*.'

The entire journey was taken up with a full account of the life of an international striptease artiste, who claimed to be the daughter of a Harley Street doctor and was *en route* for a professional engagement in Madrid. Her tale ended when she suddenly said, 'Let me hold your hand'—the pilot was starting his descent. We never met again.

MILITARY PLANNING

One morning in late May 1965, I assembled the 2nd Battalion Scots Guards in the gymnasium of the barracks at Caterham and addressed them along these lines:

Last night I was sitting at home watching the telly when the telephone rang. It was the Duty Officer in the Ministry of Defence summoning me to report at once to the office of the Chief of the Defence Staff, Lord

Mountbatten. I drove up to London at top speed, was met at the door and taken straight up.

'There is a crisis,' said the Chief. 'The Prime Minister has told me to bring you over to see him at No. 10 the moment you arrive, so all *I* can tell you now is that you must prepare your battalion for impending operations of national importance.' We then went across to Downing Street and were at once ushered in to the Cabinet Room where Mr Wilson was working, a plate of 'jam butties' by his side. 'The Commanding Officer, 2nd Battalion Scots Guards, Prime Minister,' said Lord Mountbatten.

'Sit down, Colonel,' said the PM. 'As a Scot you will know, of course, that the Isle of Mull is an independent kingdom; what you may not be aware of is that there is a treaty between HMG and the Royal Mull Government to the effect that if the latter are threatened by a foreign power, we will go to their help if requested. We have intelligence that subversive elements are about to attempt to topple the Government and that military forces of a power hostile to our country are alerted to assist these plans by committing amphibious troops on to the Island. Correct, CDS?' Lord Mountbatten nodded agreement.

'The situation in Mull is far from clear,' went on the PM, 'but it would seem that the Sovereign, King Charles the 27th (the name seems to run in the family), and his Consort, Queen Elizabeth, are confined to their castle at Duart. You are to move your battalion to Scotland forthwith and be prepared if necessary to restore the situation, as it develops on the Island. CDS, naturally, will give you all the support you require. Any questions?'

Before any could be asked, a voice from the corner of the room piped up. 'One point, Prime Minister.'

'Yes, "C"?' he replied—for 'C' was none other than the head of the Secret Intelligence Service (MI6).

'I suggest that there should be a cover plan for this operation.'

'Good idea. What do you propose?'

'I think the Battalion should be moved initially to Edinburgh, ostensibly to have a parade—say, presentation of new Colours. If they are not then to be committed immediately, they should be retained in Scotland to carry out training while the situation is monitored.'

'Quick thinking, "C",' said the PM, and turning to CDS and myself, he courteously thanked us, and we left.

108

Thus was launched a Battalion Exercise called 'Jock Scot' on Mull. The Presentation of Colours, of course, was to take place anyhow, as was the subsequent training. What, perhaps, *was* remarkable was how many members of the Battalion believed absolutely what they had been told. (Even some who were from Argyll admitted that they had not realised that Mull was an independent Kingdom!)

The local inhabitants of the island entered into the spirit of the Exercise, and on one occasion a note was found pinned upon the massive door of the Castle which read, 'Gone out shopping. Elizabeth R.'

It was the first visit of the Regiment to Mull since 1686 and the first recorded occasion that Scots Guardsmen had garrisoned Duart Castle, home of 'Chips' Maclean to whom this book is dedicated.

THE CURSE ON THE ADJUTANT

The Battalion was rehearsing for a parade at which new Colours were to be presented by the Queen. Two very senior and distinguished officers (the Quartermaster and Transport Officer) were marching together when the Adjutant sharply told them to pull their arms to the rear. A few seconds later he tripped and split his breeches.

In the Officers' Mess, after the Battalion had been dismissed, one was heard to remark to the other: 'Very satisfactory. The curse I put on him worked.'

A line of one of the hymns sung at a subsequent Battalion Service, held in St Giles Cathedral, Edinburgh, was appropriate: Courage, brother, do not stumble.

A SAD STORY OF ORNAMENTAL THISTLES

This same Scots Guards Battalion was presented with new Colours in the garden of Holyroodhouse. While we were there I noticed that on either side of the Equerries' Entrance were magnificent ornamental Scottish thistles, and I asked the Second in Command to buy a pair—at considerable expense—to be placed outside the door of the Officers' Mess at Chelsea Barracks. This was done, and daily I observed them and daily noted their ever increasing sickliness. I applied fertiliser with no effect; I sprayed the shoots which slowly drooped. The Medical Officer and the Padre were consulted to no avail.

The Irish Guards shared the barracks, and occasionally their Wolfhound visited the Mess. All was revealed. *Quis separabit?*

THE SERMON

I decided to order the entire Battalion (less Roman Catholics and 'other denominations' who were excused) to attend Divine Worship in the Guards Chapel. This was allowed by the Army Board if it was a special occasion—and I said it was, as the Commanding Officer would preach the sermon.

'There are three fundamental questions we must ask ourselves,' I said from the pulpit: 'Where have we come from?—and every time you look at a little baby, no doubt, you think that,' which, as I said it, I thought most unlikely. And then, secondly, 'And where are we going to?' and I compared life's journey to that on British Rail, but did not dwell long on this as I suddenly remembered that the destination of the traveller is clearly printed on the ticket. The third question, however, was the punch line. 'What are we here for?' and I leaned forward on the edge of the pulpit like a true clerical professional. 'Can it be to be first in the canteen queue?'

110

And, much to the fury of the Sergeant Major, a voice said, quite clearly, 'Yes!'

LIFE IN DETENTION

It was decreed that all Army Commanding Officers, together with their Adjutants and Regimental Sergeant Majors, should visit the Military Detention Centre at Colchester (sometimes called 'the Glass House'). An excellent and comprehensive programme was arranged, which covered every facet of the existence of an inmate, and at the conclusion there was an opportunity to ask questions of the Commandant.

On one such occasion, when I was the visiting Commanding Officer, I asked if there was anyone from my regiment doing 'time', and when told that there was, I requested to see him.

The soldier was produced and was asked how he was getting on.

'Oh, fine, sir,' he replied. 'It's fantastic here: smashing food, good facilities for sport, first class accommodation. In fact, sir, I prefer it to life back in the Battalion, except for one thing.'

'And what's that?'

'The walking out isn't too good!'

A SPIRITUAL REFRESHER COURSE

The Battalion was ordered to send an officer on a course at the Chaplains' Centre. The Adjutant told me that no one was available at that time, so I said he must send in a 'Nil Return'. A few days later, however, a further order arrived, saying that we *were* to send someone, and when the availability board was examined there was only one possible candidate—me!

111

So off I went, and there was a certain amount of surprise registered that I, a Lieutenant Colonel, should be attending a course for young officers. In fact there was one other student of about my age who was a Captain in the Army Pay Corps, so he and I were appointed syndicate leaders for the group discussions which featured large. (There were tricky problems posed: '. . . You are the Archbishop of Canterbury/the Moderator of the General Assembly of the Church of Scotland. What would you do?' etc.)

The Course was well run, instructive and exhausting, and so I thought I would slip away and leave the younger students to get on with it. I rose early and crept downstairs to leave for London, but I was unfortunately intercepted in the hall by a Sergeant Major in the Royal Artillery who was in charge of administration.

'Good morning, sir,' he said, 'Leaving prematurely, are we?'

'Yes, Sergeant Major,' I replied, 'a little pressing business in the Battalion requiring my immediate attention.'

'You must complete the end of course Report, sir,' he said, handing me an impressive looking form.

The top part was easy: number, rank, name, address, etc. The bottom was equally so: signature, name, etc., in block capitals. The middle part was headed, 'Course Comments', and I felt obliged to say something of moment. Accordingly I wrote, 'This Course is so good it must be made compulsory for all Commanding Officers.'

And, do you know, it was!

THE DRUM MAJOR GENERAL

'Do you think,' asked the Drum Major of the 2nd Battalion Scots Guards, as he sat in the back of a Land-Rover going up Glencoe, 'do you think, sir, that I am the Drum Major General of all England?' Such a question was just up my street.

"At the first sound of a Royal Flush we strike up with 'All Through the Night' Prestissimo!" (Prince Philip announced Windsor Castle had the noisiest toilets in the kingdom.) Cartoon by Giles. *By permission of Express Newspapers*

'Why should you be, Drum Major?'

'Well, sir, I am the Senior Drum Major in the Army; there *was* once an appointment of Drum Major General and I think it should be restored, and I am the man for the post.'

Research showed that the Drum Major was correct: there *had* been such a post up to 1830, and the last two holders had been Guardsmen. I researched further.

'Drum Major, I have been to great lengths in your cause, with no success. I cannot get anyone in authority to consider re-establishing the post but I know exactly why you wish it: no military drum could be beaten by a soldier anywhere in the Realm without the approval of competence from the Drum Major General.'

'Quite right, sir, I have already ascertained that.'

'Well, I know what you had in mind: after the 2nd Rehearsal for the Birthday Parade you would go to the Major General and tell him that the standard of drumming in the Foot Guards was of such a quality that no drum could be beaten at the Trooping.'

'Quite right, sir,' said the Drum Major. 'How did you guess?'

LAUREL LEAVES

The same Drum Major once related this tale:

When I was a young drummer stationed at Wellington Barracks, I was summoned by the Drum Major who said: 'Tomorrow is a Battle Honour Day when the Colours are wreathed with Laurels. Take this basket and go to the Electrician's gate to the garden of Buckingham Palace. Ring the bell, explain who you are and why you are there and you'll be let in. Mind you pick the laurel leaves in the garden with *long* stalks so I can make a good wreath.'

Off I went, was admitted to the garden and was about to start picking when a lady and a gentleman came round the corner.

114

'Good morning, Drummer,' said the Lady.

'Good morning, Your Majesty,' I replied.

'And what do you want?' asked Queen Mary.

'Can't you see? He's come for some laurel leaves,' said the King (for it was none other).

'Give me the basket and the King and I will pick them for you,' and they disappeared.

A short while later the Queen returned. 'Here you are. They are a nice lot,' she said, and handed me the basket. I saluted and returned to barracks.

When I gave the basket to the Drum Major, he said, 'You're a dozy individual. I told you to pick them with long stalks. These are no good!'

To which I replied, 'I didn't pick them, sir, the King and Queen did.'

'Don't give me that,' he shouted, and I was placed in close arrest and charged with Idle Picking.

8
Commander 4th Guards Brigade

Ever since the seventeenth century battalions of Foot Guards, like the Infantry of the British Army, have been grouped for operations into Brigades, and if two or more Guards Battalions were together in the same formation, it was designated a 'Guards Brigade'. Sadly this longstanding custom appears to have fallen into desuetude, but the brigade which I commanded in Germany held the old, historic title.

These random jottings fall into my period of Command.

THE BRIGADIER'S ORDERLY

I was new in post as the Brigadier, and had sent my orderly on a crash 'etiquette course' in the Mess of the Queen's Guard at St James's Palace. The orderly came from a Scottish family; indeed, his father had served in the Regiment with distinction, although the sons spoke with cockney accents.

Just before I held my first official dinner party, the orderly appeared.

'Bit of a crisis tonight, sir. I'm afraid we'll 'ave to drink the 'ock out of wine glasses.'

'Oh, I thought you *did* drink hock out of wine glasses.'

'Drink 'ock out of wine glasses? Certainly *not*. You drink 'ock out of 'ock glasses.'

Rather weakly, I could only say, 'Well, I'm sorry; we'll just have to use wine glasses, but I promise it won't happen again.'

THE TRAINING DIRECTIVE

The new Divisional Commander was extremely erudite. His first Training Directive mystified one of his Brigade Commanders (and his Chief of Staff) and contained a memorable section which read thus:

'I wish all ranks to be made aware of an important point of substance: In my opinion boundaries, be they inter Army Group, inter Corps, inter Division, inter Brigade, inter Battalion—nay, I go further—even inter Company, are distinctly *pejorative*.'

I asked my Chief of Staff to look up in the dictionary what that word meant and then to ensure that all ranks—nay, I went

117

"But, Lady Littlehampton, this all wrong — I should be drinking out of your shoe!" Cartoon by Osbert Lancaster from *Lady Littlehampton and Friends. Reproduced by permission of The Estate of Sir Osbert Lancaster and Johny Murray (Publishers) Ltd*

further—even Headquarters Company Sports storemen—were informed of the Commander's views.

THE MORGUE

I protested to the staff that the order was ridiculous, that I was quite unqualified for the task and someone more suitable should be detailed. 'Higher Authority', however, decreed that as the local British Military Hospital was in the garrison and as I was the Garrison Commander, I would carry out the annual inspection.

Came the day and, accompanied by the Commanding Officer and a forbidding Matron, I did my best, testing the scalpels in the operating theatre for sharpness, visiting the maternity ward where I jocularly assured a soldier's wife that, as a father of five, I knew it wouldn't be too bad, only to be told that she had had twins three days ago and it was awful; and chatting up the nurses.

I then came to a corridor, at the end of which stood a white-coated figure who said, 'I am the Head Pathologist,' and, flinging open an outside door and pointing with a trembling finger, added, 'Well, there it is. What do you think of it?' He was referring to a small building.

'What is it?' I asked him.

'The Mortuary.'

'I've never seen one of those before, but it looks all right, at any rate from outside.'

'All right? It's not all right at all. In the first place you can't get a stretcher through the door. The corpse falls off.' And he launched into a list of shortcomings as he showed me round.

'How long has it been like this?' I asked.

'Over 30 years.'

'But that's terrible! If it is as bad as you say, why hasn't something been done about it before?'

'I'll tell you why, Brigadier,' said the Pathologist. 'It's because

119

some idiot was stupid enough to say that the living are more important than the dead.'

He subsequently got a new morgue—and it even had a telephone in it.

THEFT

I had travelled the whole way from Münster (Westfalia) to Salt Lake City, Utah, with no mishap. On return I paused in London for breakfast in the Officers' Mess at Chelsea Barracks, leaving my suitcase in the cloakroom. When I went to collect it, it had gone.

The Regimental Police were summoned and they, in turn, called in the Metropolitan Constabulary in the shape of an efficient and zealous Detective Sergeant.

'Now, sir,' asked the latter when he had carefully recorded the circumstances of the theft. 'Can you give me any possible "lead" to the culprit?'

'Oh yes, officer. If you see a man of 6 foot 4 walking about in a lightweight tropical uniform of a Brigadier in the Scots Guards, *that* is your man.'

The detective paused and remarked, 'Now, now, sir, there's no call to be facetious,'

But, after all, it was the truth.

A CONVERSATIONAL OUTCOME

A letter in the *Journal of the Royal Army Ordnance Corps* asked why the Commander of that Corps in the London District Headquarters rode a horse, and indeed showed a photograph of the officer so mounted. No one knew the answer, but a reply came from a Brigade Commander in the British Army in Germany:

"Technically speaking, Farquharson, to the TV viewers in Moscow we're just another 'Western'."
Cartoon by Giles. *By permission of Express Newspapers*

When I was on the Staff of Headquarters London District, CRAOC (Commander Royal Army Ordnance Corps) and I were judges of the District Motorcycle competition at Pirbright. We were drinking cherry brandy in a bitterly cold hut, waiting for the approach of the contestants, with the General sitting in the corner, reading the paper.

'CRAOC,' I said, 'I know that when the Major General inspects a Battalion of Foot Guards, you are in attendance in uniform with your notebook at the ready, prepared to answer questions and so on. Where are you when he inspects the Mounted Regiment of the Household Cavalry?'

'I am in plain clothes on the touch line, as it were,' he replied.

'That's no good. You ought to be mounted and, if summoned, come forward at a hand canter, rein in, open your sabretache,[1] extract your note book, and rein back.'

At that moment the word came that the contestants were approaching and the General and the judges left.

Some weeks later I was walking across the square at Wellington Barracks, where the Household Cavalry had moved during the re-building of Knightsbridge Barracks. Emerging from the riding school I saw a hobbling figure in jodhpurs whom I identified as CRAOC.

'My dear chap, what *are* you doing?' I asked.

'It's all your fault,' came the reply. 'I'm on a ruddy equitation course.'

He was a good CRAOC. His successor was equally competent in matters Ordnance, but when, while inspecting the Household Cavalry, the Major General summoned him, he came forward at a hand canter which he failed to stop, bursting at an ever increasing speed through the Parade and disappearing from view!

A CAMP SITE

I decided to take the family on a tenting holiday in Schleswig-Holstein where we came upon a new camp site. There was only one other tent in the place and the facilities were excellent. I

---

[1] An ornately embroidered case attached to the saddle, used for carrying papers and maps.

discovered that the owner had been a Panzer Sergeant in Rommel's Afrika Korps.

'I am a panzer man myself,' I said, and a warm friendship was struck up.

'Herr General, you must come back. Ring me up and I will guarantee you a *gutes Platz*.'

Some months later, I *did* ring up the Patron. Yes, indeed, he certainly had a *gutes Platz*, and off we set. To our horror, however, on arrival the camp site was like Blackpool beach and the *gutes Platz* the size of a billiard table.

The Panzer Sergeant was delighted to see us and showed us where to go with pride. He had clearly told other campers who we were, because a crowd collected to watch the erection of the tents. The ground was rock hard and the pegs constantly buckled, causing some hilarity. One German spectator was particularly inquisitive:

'Is it so that you are in the Guards? . . . And you are a General? . . . And so you know the Queen? . . . And do you often have breakfast with Prince Charles?' . . . *und so weiter.*

At last the work was completed and, exhausted, I went to get a drink, carefully threading my way between the tents and over the ropes.

To my surprise, right in the centre of this mass of humanity sat a disconsolate figure outside a caravan: it was the Colonel of a dashing British Cavalry Regiment!

'My dear fellow, what *are* you doing here in this ghastly place?'

The Colonel smiled wanly and replied, 'Your wife recommended it.'

THE DRAG HUNT

My father-in-law, a retired Master of Foxhounds, came out to stay with us in Germany. I thought he would feel at home if I invited a German 'Drag' to meet on the local training area, and

123

this was, accordingly, arranged. I was asked by the Master to be Patron for the occasion which I accepted, delegating the riding responsibilities to one of my daughters.

A great deal of blowing of horns, consumption of liquor (at my expense) and frequent 'stops' marked the hunt's activities which culminated in a visit to a local *Gasthof* where even more liquor was provided (by me). After a while, the Master stood up, addressed the hunt and spoke of the lady rider who had, in his opinion, given the worst performance. 'The Patron,' he said, 'will step forward on her behalf.'

I did so, unaware of what was in contemplation, and found myself bent over a chair and given a crack over my posterior by the Master. I was even more put out to find myself brought forward on behalf of the male rider who had performed poorly, and given *two* whacks. This caused great hilarity and calls for more refreshment (naturally at my expense). I felt like leaving the proceedings. ('You can't,' murmured my daughter, 'whatever happens next might happen to me!')

And she was right: the performance of some wretched horse which had not come up to scratch was described in detail by the Master, and once again, amid cries of hysterical applause, the Patron was dragged forward to be thrashed *thrice*! Is it surprising that I felt luke-warm thereafter about NATO and the Common Market?

All my father-in-law (MFH North Cotswolds retd) said was, 'We don't do that sort of thing, y'know, in North Cotswold Country. Not sure about anywhere else.'

9
Experiences with the Russians

I went to Berlin shortly after the end of the War and on 11 November 1945 travelled up the *Autobahn* through the Soviet-occupied zone. At every *ausfahrt* (or exit) was a Russian Military Policewoman, directing what little traffic there was and demanding to see my credentials. All I had as a *Laissez-passer* was a canteen wine receipt, and on the strength of this I arrived to begin a six-month stay.

My work involved frequent contact with the Russians—our Soviet allies, with whom initially we enjoyed comparative trust and harmony. This, however, did not last long and shortly after I left they pulled out of the Four-Power Government of the city, and this was followed by the building of the Wall.

Later, when I had completed the course at the Imperial Defence College, to which I refer later, I returned to Germany and joined the Intelligence Community for over two years. My perspective of, and relations with, the Russians were then somewhat different.

THE PASS

My wife and some of the children gathered to see me off to work. It was my first day in the office on my appointment to the staffs of Headquarters British Army of the Rhine and NATO's Northern Army Group, and naturally I wanted to make a good impression.

'Just let's check,' said my wife. 'Spectacles? Handkerchief? Pen? Pass?'

'Pass!' I exclaimed. 'Where is it?'

'Well, I must say, that's a pretty poor start. Aren't you meant to be in charge of security?'

'Yes, of course I am. Don't just stand there. *Do* something or I'll be late!'

The family hunted everywhere. The clock ticked by, but at last a cry went up: 'Found it!' Of all improbable places it was in the pocket of my pyjamas.

'I say,' remarked one of the children, 'isn't that overdoing things a bit, having to identify yourself when you get into bed with Mother?'

A VISIT

On one occasion, while I was Head of the British Military Intelligence, Germany, I was talking to the Director of a security organisation at a cocktail party in his house.

'I want your advice,' said the Director. 'The Commander-in-Chief is visiting my Department tomorrow. What's the form? I've never had a visit like that.'

'No problem,' I said, putting down my glass. 'He's a very nice chap, you know. He'll just come into your office, and ask you if

"Ah! Scottish **Propaganda**." He found a picture of the West coast of Scotland. "I know that well." "Really, how's that?" (Pause). "I am a Submariner . . . Ha! Ha!" *Photo Public Relations Photo Section HQ 4 Div*

you've got any problems that he can help over. You'll say, "No." He'll say, "Splendid! Well done!" which will make you feel good. Then I expect he'll suggest that he should meet your staff, and before he leaves your office he'll probably run his finger along the top of a picture to see if there's dust, like this . . .'

And to demonstrate, I ran my finger over a picture in the Director's drawing room. 'And he'll say, "Yes, you'd better keep an eye on that!"' (The Director's wife was *not* amused.)

SPECIAL RELATIONS

I had only been the Head of British Military Intelligence for a week and knew almost nothing of the complex and strange world which I had entered, which had a jargon of its own. It was explained to me that I had a special relationship with the United States 'Intel Community' which was very important, and so it was no surprise when my American opposite number from Heidelberg came to see me—a man who had spent all his service working in this specialist field.

'I've got a problem,' he said, 'and would like your advice.' (*My* advice, indeed!)

'Oh yes,' I replied, 'only too pleased to help. What's the trouble?'

'Well,' he continued, 'you know the importance of All Source fusion, but we've snarled up over the integration of the PBT and the JSTP. It's got me real fixed. What do you think?'

'Yes,' I replied, 'that's quite a problem and I'd like to think a bit about it, but have you any first ideas?'

'Well,' he said diffidently, 'you may feel I'm right off course but I just wondered—er—if the answer might be—er—to set up—ah —a BBP?'

I considered his point slowly, nodded and replied: 'Funny you should say that because if I were you, that's just what I'd do.'

128

He left shortly for talks with my staff to whom he reported this conversation: 'Say, boys, that Chief of yours sure is a smart cookie!'—and I hadn't understood a single word!

A RUSSIAN OCCASION

I sought permission to hold a party in my House in Germany for the officers of the Soviet Mission (or SOXMIS) and their wives, and after considerable argument with Higher Military Authority and the Foreign Office, this request was agreed.

Immense trouble was taken to ensure that it would be a success, and every Russian speaker in the Army and Royal Air Force in Germany was asked to come and help.[1] The House Staff were briefed by the Security experts, and I personally briefed the family.

'Now don't forget that though they may well seem charming fellows—and perhaps their wives, too—remember that they are spies. So, children, do *not* say that your father leaves all the secret papers lying around or drinks too much, even if you think it's true.'

The evening came and the Home Team were all assembled. On the dot the Russians arrived led by their Chief, a very small Admiral, who at once gave presents to his hosts; he hung round the neck of my youngest daughter, aged six, a medallion.

After the reception had been going for about half an hour, this child went up to one of the British guests and said, 'I say, this party's boring—and I'm bugged!' She had clearly listened to the briefing.

---

[1] In fact the Computer went haywire and at least one Swahili speaker in the Army Catering Corps (much to his surprise) was also invited (and came).

129

Admiral Kondratyev, and the 'bugged' daughter. *Photo Public Relations Photo Section HQ 4 Div*

DEALING WITH THE RUSSIANS

An officer in the Coldstream Guards filled an appointment which looked after the foreign Defence and Military Attachés in London.

In 1966 he attended a Diplomatic Reception in the Soviet Embassy. The Orangery was thought to be bugged and Colonel Merkulov took him there to see the plants. Having positioned him by an over-large plant the Colonel (who had, it must be admitted, a great sense of humour) mentioned the Coldstreamer's name and rather slowly and precisely asked him some awkward questions.

Being wise to all their tricks, the British Officer quickly said, 'Forget about all that nonsense—have you got those secret papers you promised?' after which there was much merriment and they returned to the party, where the German Attaché was busy guzzling grapes and caviar, saying, 'The Russians would then afford one less rocket.'

At another party the Russian Colonel came up to the Coldstreamer:

'Good evening, Major, I hope you are well. Tell me who is that person over there?' pointing to the newly appointed Head of the Liaison Section.

'Ah,' said the Coldstreamer, 'that is our new boss. He is a great man with an enormous sense of humour.'

'Oh, is that so? I know all about him. He is a Lord.'

'Well, there's one thing I bet you don't know. He is related by marriage to Groucho Marx.'

'Oh, that is interesting. I did not know that.' Next day the 'Boss' had another page added to his file in Moscow.

THE RUSSIAN VISIT

I once arranged exchange visits by the Staff College Camberley and the Soviet Frunze Academy. The Commandant of the former

131

"The problem as I see it is how to convince the Russians that there's no defence against the H Bomb without letting the public get hold of any damfool idea about cutting down on generals!" Cartoon by Osbert Lancaster from *Private Views. Reproduced by permission of The Estate of Sir Osbert Lancaster and John Murray (Publishers) Ltd*

rang up, worried about the 'free' evening in the Russian programme in London:

'We've suggested opera, ballet or a concert, but all they want to do is to go to the 'Talk of the Town'. I'm not going with them by myself: it may be non-stop striptease.'

I said, really out of kindness, that I would go, too. The meal was delicious, the wines excellent and the floor show faultless. The Russian visitors clearly enjoyed it, despite the fact that a group of demonstrators who had dogged their itinerary from the moment they had arrived, had been present outside the restaurant.

As the Russians were gathered in the foyer before departure, two women rushed in and unfurled a protest banner. They were removed and the visitors departed.

'I think,' said the Commandant, 'that we ought to give those women a drink,' and so we took them (with their furled banner) to a local pub.

'This is bizarre,' murmured the Commandant. 'We have just entertained our potential enemies at considerable public expense. These women and their friends have been organised by the Metropolitan Police, telling them where to stand, and now here are you and I taking them out for a drink!'

The women were charming housewives, and just before they left to catch their last train home, one said, 'Well, see you tomorrow in Oxford.'

'Oxford?' asked the Commandant.

'Yes, that's where your visitors are going to be, isn't it?'

I was compassionate: 'I *do* admire your intelligence, but *please* not tomorrow. It's Oxford the day after.' And, as they departed, I added, 'And if you are going to do something, do it properly. Your banner was upside down and back to front!'

THE COMMANDANT AND THE ICECREAM

When the British Staff College visited the Soviet Union, led by the Commandant, they were entertained to lunch during a tour of Leningrad. The food was delicious, and the table was presided over by an officer who had a large moustache like Marshal Budyenny of World War II fame. It so happened that he was served last with every course.

The pudding was an ice-cream concoction like an American 'Knickerbocker Glory', and as time was pressing, the British Commandant told his hosts that they must leave for the next engagement the moment that all had finished this sweet—all, that is, except 'Budyenny' who was just about to start on it, with spoon poised, when the Commandant slapped him on the back, saying, 'Goodbye, Ivanovich,' and unwittingly knocked him forward so that his face was smothered with ice-cream and fruit! He had probably set back Anglo-Soviet relations by several years.

10
Director of Army Training

During my time as a soldier, I only served once in the Ministry of Defence after Commanding the 4th British Division in Germany. As Director of Training for the whole Army, I had a splendid office in the Old War Office Building in Whitehall, and it was there, on the second day of my appointment, that my Deputy asked, 'How are you going to operate?' by which he meant, when was I intending to arrive and depart each day? I enquired what had been the practice of my predecessor: I was appalled.

'Well', I replied, 'You can tell the Staff that I shall arrive at 0930 and leave at 1630—two days a week.'

He looked perplexed: 'And what about the other days?'

'Oh, I shan't be here. I shall be seeing training either in this country or abroad, and I'll be back for the two days to tell you what to do.'

He obviously thought I was mad, but that is roughly what I did for the whole time I was the Director of Army Training (or DAT)—and things got even better when I found, as his successor, an equally charming and efficient Deputy who revelled in the bureaucratic procedures of Whitehall. If a paper had to be written, he would volunteer; if a meeting had to be attended, he would postpone his leave in order to represent the Directorate. As a result, I must be one of the few officers who can honestly say that they enjoyed their spell in the Ministry.

ACTION BY THE CIVIL SERVICE

A Civil Servant found the lavatory in his Ministry blocked. He therefore took a fire bucket of water, climbed a chair and poured it into the cistern.

'Why *are* you doing that?' asked a Military colleague. 'It would be much simpler just to pour it down the loo.'

'Oh no,' came the reply, 'that would never do. You must use the proper channel!'

THE MAKING OF A MILITARY DECISION

Photographs of previous Directors of Training hung on the office walls, one of whom in 1907 was Major General, later Field Marshal Earl Haig of Bemersyde. At that time the post brought additional responsibilities for War Organisation and Home Defence. Haig was concerned about plans for expanding the Territorial Army and could not make up his mind whether it should be on a battalion or a company basis.

His sister, Henrietta, was keenly interested in spiritualism and persuaded Haig to accompany her to a séance. When the Medium had gone into a trance and was under control of a little native girl called Sunshine, she asked if anyone had a question. Haig had—and he asked whether expansion would be best conducted on a battalion or a company basis. Sunshine favoured a company basis, and that's how it was done.

This story would seem so improbable as to be untrue, had it not been recalled by Duff Cooper in his biography of Haig as fact.

A PARLIAMENTARY APPEARANCE

Ex officio, I was a member of the Defence Training Committee (DTC), along with my opposite numbers in the Royal Navy and Royal Air Force. We met under the Vice Chief of Defence Staff (Personnel and Logistics) and were tasked, amongst other things, to see whether training, which hitherto had been conducted by each Service, could in some instances be done jointly.

The training and housing of Guard Dogs was one such subject: those of the Army were at Melton Mowbray, where a rebuild of accommodation was contemplated, while those of the RAF were elsewhere. Why could they not be combined? The Committee spent hours in examination—costing, assessing efficiency, considering manpower implications and so on—and it was generally

A General off duty.

concluded that there would be no worthwhile economies achieved by a joint project.

The House of Commons Committee on Defence Expenditure decided to quiz the DTC on some of its decisions and I was detailed to justify that on the dogs. Accordingly I appeared in the Committee Room in the House and was subjected to most detailed and offensive questioning. My problem was that, *au fond*, I did not agree that the wretched dogs should be kept separate and my heart was not in my case. Matters got worse and worse, and I was sure that by the end of the day I would be removed from my post, when suddenly there was a clanger (was it the fire alarm?) and all the Members rushed out of the room for a Division of the House—and they never came back! Thus it was that the kennels were rebuilt at Melton, RAF and Army dogs remained separate,

138

and the Director of Army Training remained in his appointment, literally 'saved by the bell'.

Some years later I related this to the Secretary of State who was not at all amused!

RETRIBUTION

The Chief of the General Staff told the Adjutant General that he was displeased with the standard of fitness in the Army and something must be done. The Adjutant General told me that something *would* be done and that I, as Director of Army Training, would do it. So the slogan 'Fit to Fight' was coined, a Working Party set up, and—appropriately, I thought—Colonel Strong was appointed as Chairman.

After a few weeks I sent for the Colonel to find out how he was getting on, and all was explained.

'What about the over 50s?' I asked.

'Oh yes,' came the reply, 'they are very important. Do you know that those in that group' (and I was) 'suffer from managerial stress?'

'Really, tell me more,' and I listened with care.

When I got home, it was pouring with rain and my wife told me to put the car away.

'I can't. You are contributing to my managerial stress,' and I explained all that the Colonel Strong had said. '*You* put it away, please.'

'Not me,' said the wife, 'how old do you think I am!'

So the car stayed out. Next morning it wouldn't start: *she* got behind the wheel; *I* had to push. It was all very stressful.

139

Herr Carstens, the President of the Federal Republic of Germany, visits the Grenadier Guards on Training. He was lent a British Army pullover. "What do these mean?" he asked, looking at the badges of rank. "Your Excellency, you are a Lieutenant Colonel in the Irish Guards." "That's good," he replied, "I've never been higher than a Captain before!" (His cromach, or stick, was made in South Uist and presented to him on this occasion as he was a keen walker.) *Photo Public Relations Photo Section HQ BAOR*

L'EDUCATION PERMANENTE

I once attended a Symposium of Academics and was very impressed by the appearance of a Headmistress who addressed the meeting. She was extremely glamorous, and I murmured to my next-door neighbour that I wished I was 50 years younger. The Head said, 'At my school I believe in *l'Education permanente*, by which I mean I encourage the parents to attend classes.'

I perked up: all was not lost, and I sat next to her at lunch.

'What would you think if I rolled up at your school with a busload of Admirals, Air Marshals and Generals, all wanting to learn history?'

'Splendid,' replied the 'Good News' Head, 'but I think I should tell you that I only teach geography!'

LUNCH FOR A PERMANENT UNDER SECRETARY OF STATE

Viewers of the well known TV series *Yes, Prime Minister* are used to seeing the elite of the Civil Service taking a leisurely lunch in some distinguished St James's Club.

I once called upon a friend, who happened to be an extremely senior Permanent Under Secretary of State, in his office. I was instantly impressed by its architectural beauty, and indeed dignity, and could not but tell him how *very* suited he was to his environment.

'I imagine,' I said, 'that when the pressure is on and you are unable to go to your club for a gentle, relaxed lunch, you are able to have a little something suitable here in these charming surroundings.'

'Oh really,' he replied, 'describe, pray, the scene that you imagine.'

'Well, I would think that about ten minutes before one o'clock there is a discreet knock on the door. A very old messenger

141

wearing a slightly greened frock coat enters slowly with shuffling gait. "Your luncheon, Sir William," he says—and with gently shaking hands he places before you, on a silver salver presented by some grateful peer in the 1880s, a light collation: a plate, let us say, of wafer-thin brown bread smoked salmon sandwiches and a carafe of chilled Chablis. Yes, that's what I see.'

'Oh dear,' my friend replied, 'I'm afraid it's not quite like that.'

Aghast I said, 'Don't tell me—not a cry of "Tea's up" and a chipped enamel mug marked "Nobby"?'

And sad to relate, the Permanent Under Secretary of State admitted I was close to the mark. What would Lord Curzon have thought?

LIFE IN THE MINISTRY

It had been a come-down when I was posted from the command of a Division to the Ministry of Defence (or MOD). Admittedly, I *was* a Director, which sounded grand, but Major Generals were two-a-penny and as for Brigadiers, they just stuck on the stamps.

'I'd like my Staff Car at 12.30,' I said to my secretary on Day One.

'Staff Car? You must be joking,' she replied. 'You haven't got one. You use public transport like the rest of us.'

The jargon was novel and obscure, particularly if related to matters financial: 'Wedging up', 'Clawing back', 'Sketch Estimates', 'Long Term Costings' and 'Cash Limits' were all the rage. With regard to the last, I asked for a briefing, and a charming Civil Servant from one of the Finance Branches talked to me at length.

'I've got it! What it means is that when the money's spent, that's it. No more postings or troop movements till the next financial year.' I felt rather pleased that I'd mastered it.

MAXIMUM WIDTH
2.1 METRES (7'0")
ALL VEHICLES EXCEEDING THIS WIDTH
ARE PROHIBITED FROM ENTERING
THESE GATES
BY ORDER D.O.E.

Bureacratic madness, or a Civil Servant with a sense of humour.
Government office, Whitehall, London.

'Not quite,' he said. 'We make due provision, for example, for the Movement Vote.'

'Oh, really, how?'

'Well, for instance, we budget for Scottish soldiers stationed in battalions in the south to travel on leave to Scotland.'

'But there aren't any Scottish units in the South of England,' I replied. He looked at me in dismay.

'My word, General, you've got a bit to learn about the MOD, haven't you?'

The Major Generals (or some of us) used to meet with the Assistant Under Secretaries periodically for informal chats and we called ourselves 'No. 10 Board'. (Boards were, and probably still are, pretty fashionable in the MOD.) At least, as a result, we had some idea of what we were respectively doing or trying to do.

The following is the last Memo I ever wrote in the Ministry. It will be meaningless to most readers, but some who have served in Whitehall may feel a touch of nostalgia at the terminology.

Reference DAT/201/LM

LOOSE MINUTE

Distribution below

NO. 10 BOARD ACTIVITIES

1. On the morning of my departure from the MOD(AD), although I am under no remit to do so, I feel that I should transmit to colleagues my wishes for Christmas, which naturally can be taken to subsume those for the New Year in the general context of this minute.

2. I am, of course, aware that, in a sense, this can only be a cosmetic exercise, and time does not allow me more than a passing reference to the general requirement for individuals to address themselves to a point of financial substance: wedging up

in relation to the Festive Pause will almost certainly necessitate at least a token estimate to compensate for the clawing back which, in my submission, prudence might dictate as being desirable (but by no means inevitable) at the turn of the year—that is to say the calendar year.

3. I acknowledge that I have expressed this somewhat crudely, but presentationally I trust that, subject ultimately to Ministerial approval, colleagues will be content to let matters stand, but not too still.

19 Dec 78   DAT

Distribution
Action:
DMO
DASD
ACGS(OR)
DCD(A)
VAG
VQMG
DPR(A)
DMGO

Information:
AUS(GS)
AUS(AQ)

11
Scotland

When I was a boy, I remember walking down Princes Street and looking up at Edinburgh Castle where the Governor's personal Standard flew. I used to think, 'What a swell must live there,' little knowing that one day I would become that 'swell'. For any Scot and any soldier it was a thrill to be appointed to command 'the Army in Scotland' and to be the Governor of Her Majesty's Castle where my wife and I resided in apartments from after Hogmanay till the end of March. It would be difficult to imagine a more romantic setting: after dinner we would put on boots and coats and go outside. And then we would walk around the snow-covered, floodlit battlements with the music of the Pipes in the background, looking out over the twinkling lights of the New Town and across the water to Fife.

Here are some jottings which seem to me to be typically Scots or associated with that country in general and, in some cases, Edinburgh in particular.

A JOHN BROWN VIGNETTE

General Sir Lyndoch Gardiner was one of Queen Victoria's Equerries and when Sir Frederick Ponsonby (Fritz) joined the Royal Household in 1894 he was aged eighty and becoming forgetful. Ponsonby recalls the following:

On one occasion, when coming into Waiting, he asked John Brown, Queen Victoria's personal Scottish Attendant, how Her Majesty was and what she had been doing lately. Brown replied: 'The Queen's verra weel. It was only the other day that she said to me, "There's that dommed auld fool General Gardiner coming into Waiting and I know he'll be putting his bluidy nose into everything that doesn't concairn him!" '[1]

A VISIT TO THE ACADEMY

I do not come from a military family. All my forebears were artists, musicians and academics, and although I do not paint myself, I like pictures.

One day I visited the Royal Scottish Academy in Edinburgh, and in one of the galleries I noticed a man looking at a large portrait through his hands which he held up to make an 'O', and wondered why he was doing it, but dismissed the thought.

Some time later I remembered what I had seen and went up to a picture and did the same. A female visitor tapped me on the shoulder and said, 'Do tell me: I've always wanted to know. Why are you doing that?'

I replied, quite truthfully: 'Madam, I have no idea.' The lady left in haste to escape from this lunatic.

[1] *Recollections of Three Reigns.* Sir Frederick Ponsonby. Macmillan London.

PAUL MAZE

He was 92 years young when he died, and quite apart from being an outstanding artist, he was the most remarkable man I have ever met. His sense of fun was one of his characteristics and is illustrated by these two anecdotes:

The dealer Alfred Daber remembers one of Maze's practical jokes. He had taken Lord Sandwich and the Archbishop of Canterbury, Lang, to visit his friend, the artist Segonzac, in Paris as they both wanted to have an *aperçu* of the artist's way of life. They were given cheese and bread for dinner and were made to help wash the dishes. As they were leaving Maze told them that one of the essential duties in an artist's life was to take down the dustbins at night. He gave one to each visitor and sent them down while he locked up. As he followed them down, he heard screams from the *concierge* as the poor Archbishop had dumped the lot on

His Royal Highness nearly makes an 'O'. The Prince of Wales visits Paul Maze's exhibition and is shown round by the artist. *Photo Central Press/Photo Source*

her doorstep. 'Haven't you learnt yet where to put these wretched things?' she shouted at the terrified cleric who was endeavouring to escape with what little dignity he could still command.

When Paul worked from the studio in Paris, he produced mainly still lifes and nudes. Indeed, he and Derain shared for their work a black model called Fifi. Maze enjoyed telling the story of an impromptu visit from a family solicitor, which forced him to shut Fifi in the tiny cupboard-like kitchen. He feared that a view of the naked black girl might offend the sensibilities of the bowler-hatted lawyer. As luck would have it, the visitor asked for a cup of tea, so Maze characteristically told him that there was some ready in the kitchenette, and pointed to the door. When he went through, the startled lawyer found, not tea, but the grinning Fifi sitting on the stove.

THE ATHOLL HIGHLANDERS

Described by the present Duke as 'our so-called private army', the Atholl Highlanders are unique. In its present form, the Regiment dates from 1839, and three years later formed a Guard of Honour for Queen Victoria and Prince Albert at Dunkeld. In 1843 it mustered four Companies, each of 40 Highlanders, the Right Flank Company being equipped with the Lochaber axe, each man over six feet tall. When Her Majesty and the Prince Consort stayed at Blair in 1844, the Highlanders mounted the Castle Guard daily, and two artillery pieces were added to fire salutes.

The Queen presented the first Colours in 1845, and Mrs Butter, the wife of the Adjutant, the second in 1966.

This flourishing and enthusiastic body is about one hundred strong, with pipes and drums.

The following correspondence deals with their armament.

MEMORANDUM

To: Major D.H. Butter, MC,   20th June 1980
     Adjutant, The Atholl Highlanders,
     Cluniemore, Pitlochry.

WEAPONRY

Sir,

1. I have the honour to inform His Grace the Colonel, Atholl
    Highlanders, through you that I have received a request for
    new weaponry to be acquired for the Regiment under His
    Grace's command.
2. I have set in train the necessary arrangements for this to be
    done, and accordingly 70 rifles No. 4 (point 303 inch) with
    welded bayonets can (and will be) provided on condition that
    confirmation is received from you or an officer authorised by
    you before 22nd July 1980.
3. I am confident that this issue of new weaponry will contribute
    to the smartness and efficiency of the only military unit in
    Scotland that does not come under the command of

Your obedient servant,

J. M. GOW

Lieutenant-General
General Officer Commanding The Army in Scotland
and Governor of Edinburgh Castle

Silent Copy to: CRAOC.

The Atholl Highlanders. Three new recruits being presented with juniper sprigs to wear in their bonnets upon enlistment. The tall figure of His Grace the Colonel is seen on the right, with Colour Sergeant Willie Ross carrying his personal Standard. Behind the recruits stands Sergeant Major James Stewart, who joined the Highlanders in 1966 and was appointed Sergeant Major in 1971. The two guns were last used to fire a salute in 1968 when two ex-Royal Artillerymen (one of whom was the Sergeant Major) used too large a charge too near the castle and broke 18 panes of glass! *Photo Atholl Highlanders collection*

151

Confidential & Personal

CLUNIEMORE,

PITLOCHRY,

SCOTLAND.

PITLOCHRY 2006.

3 0th June, 1980.

Lt-General Sir Michael Gow, KCB,
G.O.C. Army Scotland,
Army Headquarters,
Edinburgh EH1 2YX.

Sir,

1. I have the honour to acknowledge receipt of your welcome Dispatch concerning the supply of new Weaponry for the Atholl Highlanders.

2. I am instructed by the Colonel, His Grace The Duke of Atholl, to thank the General Officer Commanding for his solicitous attention to this important matter, and to confirm that His Grace wishes the full implementation of same at your earliest convenience.

3. His Grace has also asked me to say that with the advent of new Weaponry the improved smartness and efficiency of his Army will doubtless justify the confidence expressed in your Dispatch. His Grace would like to add that the General Officer Commanding is assured that these weapons will be in much safer and more reliable hands than if they had been disposed of in the open market in the Middle East.

I have the honour to be, Sir

Your Obedient Servant,

David. H. Butler .

Adjutant, The Atholl Highlanders.

152

THE PROTEST

While we were living in Edinburgh Castle, I had occasion to chide one of my daughters:

"You are pathetic. If the Americans put a foot wrong, you and your friends are up in arms at once. But what are *you* doing about Soviet dissidents? What about Afghanistan? Nothing!'

I then went away on tour and, on my return, my wife said, 'Listen to this.' I opened the sitting room door and heard, 'Hello, is that you, Doctor Bukovsky? This is the Scottish organiser of the Movement in Defence of Human Rights . . .' Impressed, I asked her what she had in mind.

'A Silent Vigil,' she suggested.

'Difficult if silent, no one will know when it has started or ended,' I replied. After long debate, she decided upon a demo on the Mound, for which I would provide the stand and loud hailer.

It was reported that Dr Bukovsky said in Trafalgar Square, London, 'At this very moment, our comrades in Scotland are rallying with us.' It was, in a sense, true, because my daughter *was* standing on her box on the Mound, with a loud hailer, backed by a banner which read 'Russians out of Afghanistan'. And a Scot who had well sustained himself over luncheon said to her, 'Quite right, my dear, and we want to get those ruddy English oot of Scotland too.'

Edinburgh Castle. The Regimental Band Scots Guards and Pipes and Drums on the Esplanade.

12
The Queen's Body Guard for Scotland

The Royal Company of Archers is an august body, over 300 years old, and is the Scottish equivalent of the English Honourable Corps of Gentlemen-at-Arms. It is, however, much larger, numbering about four hundred Archers, all of whom apply to be elected, a process which takes anything up to seven years. The Royal Company is commanded by the Captain General, who is also the Gold Stick for Scotland, and, in descending order of seniority, the Officers are Lieutenants, Ensigns and Brigadiers. They parade in Scotland whenever required to be in attendance on the Sovereign, and a high standard of shooting with the long bow, with which they are equipped, is maintained by an annual shoot for the Queen's Prize and a competition against the Woodmen of Arden, a distinguished English Shooting Society.

ON BECOMING AN ARCHER

Sir Alastair Blair recalls: 'On my very first rehearsal parade a late lamented member of the Royal Company welcomed me warmly as a last-joined and very frightened recruit. He then went on, "I expect you know most of these chaps already; but anyhow it's easy seeing that the Royal Company is recruited from the criminal classes." I recognised several distinguished Admirals and Generals within easy earshot . . .'

LINES WRITTEN IN
CONTEMPLATION OF THE KING'S BODY GUARD
FOR SCOTLAND—1937

Between the Palace and the Hill
Behold the ranks of Archers stand
They are not standing straight or still
And yet the spectacle is grand.

Upon their bosoms, row by row,
Medals acquired in warfare shine;
Look, there's a lad who fought the foe
(Six clasps) in 1889.

And there are other medals too
Won from the battle strife afar.
This man's a Fellow of the zoo
And that's an OBE (with bar).

The Adjutant has called out "Shun!"
What do they care? 'It's only Cis,'[1]
And through the serried ranks there run
Fragments of dialogue like this:

[1] The Adjutant, Brigadier, Lieutenant-Colonel N. V. C. Dalrymple-Hamilton.

'Have you got heather-beetle still?'
'This year the plovers' eggs were late.'
'What do you think of Herbert's bill?'
'My God! I've dropped my dental plate!'

But yet the Monarch proudly knows
In gazing on this noble Corps
That he is guarded by those bows
Which few can hold and fewer draw.[1]

IN THE GARDEN OF HOLYROODHOUSE

During the Queen's Garden Party, an American guest said to a member of the Royal Company of Archers on duty in Her Majesty's lane: 'Say, can I ask you a question? Are youse guys a mobile group or are you local?'

A REHEARSAL

The Queen was about to present new Colours to her Body Guard for Scotland and the Captain General sensibly considered that some rehearsals would be beneficial. Accordingly the Adjutant, himself a Grenadier, had a Drill Sergeant from his Regiment sent up to Edinburgh to put the Royal Company through their paces.

On one such occasion, he took the officers behind the gymnasium at Redford Barracks for private tuition. These gentlemen were all extremely distinguished—Admirals, Generals, several Knights of the Thistle and many Peers of the Realm.

---

[1] Anon. Quoted by Ian Hay in his *History of the Royal Company of Archers.* William Blackwood, 1951.

A Holyroodhouse Garden Party. "Talking to an Archer on duty is not allowed." *Photo The Scotsman Publications Ltd*

Sword drill was the subject, and the Drill Sergeant was heard to remark to a very senior officer, 'Come, come, sir, the way you march carrying your sword, you might be tip-toeing upstairs holding a candle!'

LATE FOR PARADE

As a member of the Queen's Body Guard for Scotland, I was detailed for duty at the Palace of Holyroodhouse at a Reception given by the Queen after a banquet. 'Now, whatever you do,' the

The Queen's Body Guard for Scotland (The Royal Company of Archers).
Photo George Outram & Co Ltd

Adjutant said, 'don't be late. We will parade in the Palace Forecourt.'

Come the evening, I made a particular point of punctuality, but when I arrived and got out of the car, holding bow and bonnet, no one was about! Heavens! I couldn't surely be late? I saw a policeman. 'Have you seen anyone around like me?'

'No,' said the officer, 'but gang awa through that door and ye may get help.' And so I did, climbed some stairs and opened a door at the top.

A splendid sight met the eyes. The High Constables of Holyroodhouse were sitting at a large table upon which were decanters of liquid amber and glasses. The scene was convivial and pleasing.

'Hello,' one cried, 'we haven't had one of you up here for ages. Sit down and have a dram.' Not one to refuse hospitality, I did so,

159

and the beverage and hilarity flowed merrily till the door opened and the Constable's face peered in.

'Ye're required,' he said. 'The officer's nae best pleased, I'm thinking.' I was, alas, late again.

RIGOURS OF A ROYAL RECEPTION

The scene was the same Reception:

'You will stand here, in this alcove, with grace, adding general distinction to the proceedings until I give you further instructions.' Thus spake the Adjutant, and so I stood for what seemed to me a very long time. Her Majesty's guests entered. They conversed and sustained themselves. The Moderator of the General Assembly of the Church of Scotland stood within three feet of me, enjoying the Royal Hospitality. After a while, I confess the flesh succumbed.

'Moderator,' I pleaded, 'would you mind moving on. Unlike Lazarus, I am not allowed even to pick up the crumbs!'

TRICKY MANOEUVRES

It is a great honour to be appointed an officer in the Royal Company, but there I was, a Brigadier which is the most junior rank (and I was the most junior Brigadier).

The scene: a rehearsal for a Garden Party at Holyroodhouse. My superior officer (an Ensign) is briefing the Archers.

'Right, pay attention. First point: if you feel "peely wally", fall out and be treated. Do *not* faint, so go when you are "peely" and before "wally".

'Next what you have to do is simple except for two manoeuvres which last year were *very* badly done and we don't want a repeat, do we?' All nodded in agreement. 'Now, the first is when the

160

Queen and Members of the Royal Party enter the tea tent. The circle of Archers, holding back the guests, contracts to make a smaller space before the Tent. Those not required are formed up and marched off to join the rest of the Royal Company. Tricky. The General (me!) will be in charge of all that.

'Next the very last Archers in the circle must quickly be formed up *after* the Queen has left the tent but before the Household and guests, and smartly moved to fall in with all the others. Got it? *Very* difficult and it easily can be a shambles. The General will be in charge of that, too.'

At that time in my military career I commanded three-quarters of a million men from five different nations, but those manoeuvres were infinitely more difficult to execute.

The incident was recorded in the following exchange, reminiscent perhaps of the Field Marshal Alexander-Montgomery correspondence:

'Chips' Maclean commanding the Queen's Escort of Archers at Holyroodhouse, Edinburgh.

161

Dear Alex,

It was an honour and a privilege to serve under your Command on the occasion of my first commissioned duty. As you had appreciated, there were two most critical moments in 'the Circle', and in respect of both you placed me clearly in command. As I remarked to the Adjutant, if they could be described as the Alam Halfa and El Alamein of the 1981 Holyroodhouse Garden Party, we have surely made a mark in the annals of the Royal Company.

Yours ever,

Monty

Dear Monty,

I was delighted to receive your letter. It was apparent that the Supreme Commander was satisfied with our mutual effort to control the approach of the invaders. Your handling of the withdrawal from the outer circle was masterful, bringing the invaders well within range of the strawberry-and-cream-throwers in the command vehicle should an onslaught have ensued.

When the history of the Queen's Body Guard is written again, all will be revealed.

Happy combat, my dear Monty—with best wishes until our next combined operation.

Your admiring,

Alex

THE ENTRY OF THE QUEEN

A Brigadier of the Royal Company was briefing his detachment as to their duties in the High Kirk of St Giles on the occasion of a Service of the Order of the Thistle:

162

'Now, pay attention. When you have taken up the positions that I have indicated, you stand easy. You first come to attention when Her Majesty enters with "Zadok the Priest".'

'Zadok the Priest!' exclaimed an Archer. 'What's he doing here?'

ROBBERY

Soon after her arrival in Kenya, my wife and I went on safari to Uganda. The very next night our house was broken into and almost all our possessions were stolen. Only one item was recovered, and on that hangs this tale.

I was summoned to appear as a witness in the magistrate's court in Nairobi, and when the case was called, into the dock stepped one of the toughest and most sinister Africans I had ever seen. He was charged with being one of the gang that had 'turned over' our house, and when I was summoned to the witness box, the Prosecuting Counsel held up a tie.

'Is this your property?' he asked, and the item was handed to me for identification. 'Yes, sir,' I replied, and Counsel said to the Beak that it had been found in the accused's house. It was, he implied, a cut and dried case.

Defending Counsel then rose. 'Has this tie got your name on it?' he asked.

Answer: 'No,' and I added that it merely had the name of a haberdashery in Scotland. Counsel considered the last to be an irrelevance (which perhaps it was, but I was only trying to be helpful).

'Would you not agree that this is a brightly coloured tie?'

Answer: 'Yes.'

'I put it to you that this is just the sort of tie that my client might quite legimately own.'

'Sir,' I answered, 'if that were so, I should be obliged to write to the Captain General complaining about the standard of admission of members to the Queen's Body Guard, The Royal Company of Archers, for *that* is our tie!' (*Laughter in Court.*)

That clinched it. How long the accused was sent down for I cannot now recall, but the effect was salutary and we were not robbed again.

13
Tales of the Kirk

I was brought up in a deeply religious household where prayers were said before breakfast—and everyone attended; I went to Sunday morning Service, Sunday School and sometimes Evensong as well. As a child, while I had my supper, the Bible was read to me, and I clearly remember a particularly gloomy picture of a stormy sky of black clouds through which, in a gap, an eye gazed down. The caption read, 'God seeth all,' which guaranteed me a sleepless night.

Nevertheless my devotion to the Kirk, of which I am an Elder, is firm, and tales of Ministers, their doings and sayings have always amused me.

A MILITARY GRACE

After Beating Retreat by the Massed Pipers on the Esplanade the following Grace was said before the subsequent dinner:

Oh Lord, we cease our endless chatter to think on things that really matter.

After those splendid pipes and drums, we now proceed to fill our tums.

For food and friends and *joie de vie*, we give our thanks, O Lord, to thee.

A MINISTER'S GRACE AT BALMORAL

A Minister of the Church, when asked to say Grace before dinner, bowed his head and said, 'God bless our food; God bless our wine; and God bless our intercourse tonight.'

Queen Victoria might well have been amused.

A ROMAN CATHOLIC FATHER'S GRACE IN GERMANY

'Rub-a-dub-dub, thank God for our Grub. Amen.'

OFFICIAL ADVICE

In the Summer of 1941 the Rt. Rev. the Bishop of Fulham recorded in a letter to *The Times*: 'A few weeks ago I was given official advice as to what action to take in a gas attack. I was recommended to put both my hands in my pockets and if I carried an umbrella to put it up.

This morning (June 3) the President of the Board of Trade told me on the wireless that if I found myself without any clothes owing to a "blitz" I should appear before the Local Assistance Board and demand coupons. It is puzzling . . .'

THE MIRACLE

The Minister decided to preach on miracles, and to illustrate the thrust of his sermon he held up a flower bulb. 'Look at this,' he said, 'is it not a miracle that this bulb can turn into a beautiful tulip?'—and he held up a really lovely flower.

As the congregation departed, one of them said to him, 'I liked that sermon about Miracles,' and the Minister was duly gratified. 'Yes,' the parishioner said, 'the way you turned that daffodil bulb into a tulip was truly miraculous.'

THE KIRK

When a battalion of the Scots Guards arrived in a large base in Malaysia, there was a Church of England Church but no Kirk. The Commanding Officer, therefore, ordered the Quartermaster to expropriate a barrack hut and convert it, and this was done.

Accompanied by the Adjutant, the Padre, the Quartermaster and Sergeant Major, he decided to inspect it when it was reported

167

that work was completed. When he entered, on the wall behind the Communion table was written in bold letters, 'SCOTLAND FOR EVER'.

'That won't do, will it?' He asked, looking generally round at his entourage. 'Do something about it and I'll come back tomorrow.'

The next day, the same party went back, to be met by the Pioneer Sergeant. 'All right now?' asked the Commanding Officer.

'No problem, sir,' the latter replied, and in they went. There on the wall were the words, 'SCOTLAND FOR EVER AND EVER, AMEN'.

CONVERSION

The Roman Catholic Army Padre was a delightful and most amusing man. Quite apart from being a first class Priest, he played a good hand at Bridge and mixed a particularly strong and excellent dry martini.

My mother took a liking to him, and one day enquired of him how it was that he had become a Padre.

'Well,' he replied, 'I completed my time as a National Service Officer in the Irish Guards and I decided to get a job in the City. I had a flat in Lower Sloane Street and daily I took the underground to work. It must have been somewhere between Victoria and St James's Park Station that I got "the Call".'

'How *very* interesting,' she remarked. 'The power of the Lord must be extremely strong to penetrate as deep as that.' And she was absolutely serious, too, and had not sampled one of his cocktails.

THE PADRE'S HOMILY

The Padre decided to talk to the Guardsmen about Moral Courage and gave, as his example, a barrackroom where, just before 'Lights Out', all the men jumped into bed except one, who knelt down to say his prayers.

'Now there is a demonstration of what I mean,' he said. 'Can any of you think of another example?'

There was a long, somewhat embarrassing pause, at the end of which, no doubt prompted by the watchful Sergeant, a Guardsman said, 'Yes, sir. Imagine a room full of Ministers. At nightfall, all kneel to say their prayers, except one, who jumps into bed. He is showing moral courage!'

A PREACHER'S ALTERCATION

A Minister of Cumbernauld many years ago was noted for a very disjointed and rambling style of preaching. On one occasion the Minister called upon the beadle to 'wauken my Lord Elphinstone', whom he noticed was having a snooze.

'I'm no sleeping, Minister,' Lord Elphinstone said.

'Indeed you were, my Lord. What had I been saying last then?'

'Oh, just "wauken Lord Elphinstone".'

'Ay, but what did I say before that?'

'Indeed,' retorted Lord Elphinstone, 'I'll gie ye a guinea if ye'll tell that yerself, Minister.'[1]

---

[1] This story, and the following three, are taken from *Reminiscences of Scottish Life and Character* by Dean Ramsay. Edmonston & Co, Edinburgh, 1877.

JOTTINGS IN A GENERAL'S NOTEBOOK

PREPARATION FOR CONFIRMATION

A boy visited the Minister for examination before receiving his first Communion and was asked how many Commandments there were. He replied, cautiously, 'A hunner.' The Minister was not pleased and told him that he would have to wait and learn more, so he went away.

On returning home he met a friend going to the Manse, also for examination, and he shrewdly asked him, 'Well, what will ye say noo if the Minister speers hoo many Commandments there are?'

'Say? Why I shall say ten, to be sure.'

To which the other rejoined, with triumph, 'Ten! Try ye him wi' ten! I tried him wi' a hunner and he wasna satisfied.'

HEAVEN

When told of Heaven, a small Scot asked his teacher, 'An' will faather be there?' She answered that of course she hoped he would be, to which he replied, 'Then I'll no gang.'

SABBATH OBSERVATION

An Elder of the Kirk found a little boy and his sister playing marbles on Sunday.

'Boy, do ye know where children go to who play marbles on Sabbath-day?'

'Ay,' said the boy, 'they gang down to the field by the water below the brig.'

'No,' roared out the Elder, 'they go to Hell and are burned.'

The little boy, really shocked, called to his sister, 'Come awa', Jeannie, here's a man swearing awfully.'

SUPERNATURAL VENGEANCE

A local builder came to mend the roof after a great storm. 'The wrath of the Lord has descended upon the heads of the ungodly, Bertie.'

'Quite right, sir, just what I said to my wife, but she said, "Don't mention it to the General".'

PENITENCE

My telephone in Germany rang: the caller was an old friend, a retired Major General now Clerk to the Dean and Chapter of Windsor. After an exchange of pleasantries the caller asked if the C-in-C (me) ever came to England. When an affirmative was given, he asked further, 'Are you by any chance over on . . . ?' (and he gave a date).

'Curiously enough, I am,' I said.

'Doing anything that evening?'

And thinking my friend was about to suggest a convivial soirée, I replied, 'No, actually, I'm free.'

'Oh, good,' said the Clerk, 'the Dean will be delighted. He wants you to speak in St George's Chapel. Timings will follow'—and he rang off.

Time passed, and during a major NATO exercise a member of my staff, sitting in a car in a dripping, Westfalian wood, telephoned the Dean, who was out; was transferred to one of the Canons-in residence, who was absent but his daughter answered.

'My boss is all set to speak. His subject is "The place of the Army in Society".'

'That's no good,' said the daughter. 'The Dean won't have that. We expect him to talk on Penitence—and with particular reference to washing of feet.'

I was appalled, and summoned my chief religious adviser who

171

was even more so. (*The Oxford Dictionary* is a little vague on 'Penitence'.)

Come the day, I visited an old friend in the Lower Ward of the Castle, who was a Military Knight and who prescribed a glass of liquid amber to the speaker (and himself) to prepare both for the ordeal ahead—and then, as the first was merely a 'warmer into the bank', glasses were recharged. Together we went to the Chapel. I was introduced by the Dean and launched into my address; the Knight sat in the front row, clasping a bowler hat to his chest, and within two minutes was fast asleep. I have never been invited again!

A MILITARY DEAN

The former Dean of Windsor and I were contemporaries at Sandhurst in the War. He was a Cavalryman, and as a historian his knowledge of the accomplishments of that Arm is profound. (I relate the following anecdote because of our friendship and shared sense of humour).

I once accompanied him on a lecture tour of the field of the Battle of Waterloo (1815) where he spoke eloquently. As we embussed to move to the Chateau of Hougomont where I was to speak of the action of the Foot Guards, one of the party said, 'Surely there were other soldiers taking part in the battle other than the Cavalry?'

He was, of course, right: at my 'stand' no cavalryman took part at all (except a solitary Sergeant in my own Regiment who unhorsed a French Colonel, mounted himself and rode back through the gates). I confess I may have spoken with a touch too much enthusiasm. Indeed, I was gratified to note a female listener to my words mopping her eyes as I got into my stride (I discovered that she was not so moved by my words: she suffered from hay fever).

172

I was told later that one of the 'Group' called at the Deanery in Windsor Castle and said how interested he had been during the tour.

'I'm so glad,' said the Dean. 'Of course, Mike Gow overdid it a bit, didn't you think?'

14
C-in-C BAOR and COMNORTHAG

When I was posted for the last time in my military career to Germany, I filled two appointments, one national, as Commander-in-Chief British Army of the Rhine, and the other international, as Commander of the Northern Army Group of NATO. I was stationed in the large Headquarters of Rheindahlen, not far from München Gladbach, where I had also filled dual appointments previously as Head of Intelligence and Security (or Counter Intelligence) for the United Kingdom and NATO. When, on that occasion, I had finished my tour of duty and handed over to my keen successor, I drove slowly past the Headquarters building with my family. It was a very hot day and the car was loaded with luggage and dogs. The staff officers were returning to work after lunch, striding forwards purposefully with set, determined faces. I could not resist the temptation and I opened the window and made what I believe in police reports is called 'an obscene gesture'.

'Why are you waving at those chaps?' asked one of my children.

'Because I will *never* come back,' I replied. How wrong I was.

On my last posting I was there for nearly three years and the following jottings relate to that time.

AN INVITATION

I once received a letter from the Secretary of what I considered to be about the most obscure Dinner Club I could imagine, inviting me to come as their Guest of Honour. I was about to decline when I noticed the letters 'PTO' at the foot of the page. I turned it over and the Secretary had written: 'You may be interested to see some of those who have been our Guests of Honour in the past.' To my surprise I saw names such as Kitchener, Haig, Jellicoe, Trenchard, Montgomery . . . So I replied, accepting.

The Secretary wrote with the administrative instructions, adding how pleased he was. 'Many of our members are coming to the Evening of their Lives'—which I assumed to be *the* social event of the year in their calendar. How wrong I was. I was easily the youngest person present at the dinner.

COMMENT ON A NEW STYLE UNIFORM

Like all the other soldiers in the Formation, I was issued with a new pattern, camouflaged combat uniform. I took it home and tried it on.

'Do you think this fits?' I asked my wife.

'Why are you dressed like that?' interrupted one of the children.

'If the Enemy looked at me, they would think I was a tree.'

'Yes,' she replied, 'and when they saw your moustache they would think there was a bird's nest in the branches!'

The 'Tree and the Bird's Nest'.

A RELIGIOUS INTERVAL

The Commandant of the British Garrison in Berlin took a visiting friend to church one Sunday. Before the Service started he said, 'You know, we can leave halfway through if we want to.'

'Really,' said his friend. 'How do you know that?'

'It says so in the Order of Service Sheet. Look.' The visitor did.

'No, no,' he replied, 'that doesn't say "intermission", it says "intercessions"!'

A CONCERT

The same Commandant took the same friend to a concert in Berlin. In the interval, the former remarked: 'I rather liked that catchy little Russian tune the orchestra played, didn't you?' His friend, mystified, looked at the programme.

'No, no!' he replied. 'You've been looking at next week's programme'—and the Commandant had!

Let there be no misunderstanding, however: the Commandant was an outstanding General, intelligent and highly decorated.

AIR TRAVEL AND ITS HAZARDS

The Commander-in-Chief, Royal Air Force Germany, allowed me to make use of an aircraft of the liaison flight, called a Pembroke. It was said that these two-engined planes were older than the pilots who flew them.

On one occasion I was travelling back to England with my wife who is a nervous flier, particularly when 'turbulence' is experienced. On this trip it was, and as we crossed the Channel we were thrown

Two fellow Divisional Commanders roughing it 'in the field' during manoeuvres in Germany. On the right: The Commander 1st Armoured Division (later Chief of the General Staff and a Fieldmarshal). On the left: The Commander 4th Armoured Division, talking to their mutual boss, the Corps Commander (who was somewhat surprised by this hilarity on an occasion which was part of the Great Deterrent).

about the sky in a very alarming way. As we passed over the Kent coast, however, the atmospheric conditions became genial, but my wife suddenly asked, 'Why has that engine stopped?'

Quick as a flash I replied, reassuringly, 'Fuel economy. Don't you know that the country is facing a grave economic crisis?'

This seemed to placate my wife, unlike another female passenger who was an air traffic controller at an RAF base and who, unbeknown to us, was sitting in a separate compartment between us and the flight deck. She told me later that she had been listening to the talk on the radio and suddenly heard a 'May Day'

Departure from Berlin. "Fasten your safety belts, ready for take-off."

distress call over the air. She wondered what the luckless aircraft was until suddenly realising that it was us!

Thanks to the skill of our crew, we just reached Northolt and stopped after an unusually short 'taxi'. At once we were surrounded by fire engines, staff cars with important and anxious looking officers—and there was even an ambulance.

My wife and I were taken rapidly to the VIP lounge and given suitable sustenance.

179

'What would have happened if the other engine had stopped?' she asked the Wing Commander (Ops).

Without batting an eyelid, he replied, 'No problem. You see these planes are specially designed to glide over long distances.' And she believed every word!

A QUESTION OF IDENTIFICATION

I decided to fly back to Germany from an airfield near my home in England, the entrance to which was controlled by a Ministry of Defence policeman. The car was stopped, evidence of identity, quite properly, requested and given. The policeman studied it for some time.

'That's all right, Mr Brown,' he said at last.

'Mr Brown,' I said. 'Who's he?'

'You,' came the reply, 'it says so on your card.'

'That's not my name, that's the colour of my hair!'

THE AMBASSADOR'S RECEPTION

The Ambassador's guest was standing at an informal evening reception in the courtyard of His Excellency's home in Brussels, and was momentarily by himself. A guest arrived somewhat late. He was a Polish émigré Count, and he said to the guest, 'I understand there is an important British General here tonight.' The guest murmured that he gathered that also.

'You', said the Count, 'are either the General or the butler.'

'And which, sir, do you think I am?'

'The butler, and I'd like a large glass of whisky!'

By a curious coincidence some time later, the General (and it was I) was relating this story to the Belgian Ambassador to the Court of St

NATO in action. Commander of the 1st Belgian Corps (*right*): "Do not worry, *Mon General*. All will be well. Come! A little *aperitif*, I think."

181

James, and to a man to whom he had not been introduced. 'I know who that was,' the latter said, 'it was my brother!'

A MEDICAL OPINION

I had just got through a particularly unpleasant disease. One of my children found a medical dictionary and looked it up.

'I say,' she announced, 'just listen to this. It says here: "This disease has a high mortality rate or it can do irreparable damage to the brain." Well, he's still here, so he must be round the bend!'

THE PHYSICAL FITNESS TEST

The Chief of the General Staff was worried by the high mortality rate of his General Officers (in peacetime) and decreed that they would all be subjected to a series of medical examinations and tests of a comprehensive character. Accordingly I clocked in at the largest military hospital in the country, where a few months later I found myself, quite coincidentally, as an inmate. The final test was vigorous.

'Right. Get on that treadmill. Do not look up or down, left or right, and keep moving.'

By a brilliant piece of deduction, I looked to my front, through a window to the outside world, upon which I gazed as I trudged. The trudge developed into a canter and would have ended in a gallop, had it not been stopped. I had been wired up to some machine, and the specialist was gazing with pursed lips at the cardiograph.

'A bit of concern here, General. Note this sudden change in pattern here. Nothing to be alarmed about, maybe, but . . . ?'

I could have told him the cause, but it was so elementary. As I trudged, etc., a small crowd had collected outside and watched

The Army medical authorities attributed the high mortality rate among the Generals to excessive extramural commitments. *Photo Public Relations Photo Section HQ 4 Div*

me through the window. One of their number I recalled particularly: he wore a very large, flat tweed cap which rested upon his ears, pushing them downwards. It was he who had shouted out (much to the amusement of the others), 'Keep going, Guv! I 'spect it'll kill you. Ha! Ha!' No wonder I had a tremor.

183

July 1983. The
Commander in Chief
leaves his official
residence in Germany
on relinquishing his
command.

THE LAST MANOEUVRE

Five minutes before the Exercise was due to end, I assembled my
staff.

'Gentlemen, this is the last manoeuvre I shall take part
in during my long military career.'

German Chief of Staff: 'Sir, you must be very sad.'

'Sad! I am absolutely thrilled!'

B 4160 CinC

The Chief of the General Staff
Ministry of Defence (Army)
Main Building
Whitehall
LONDON SW1   1 July 1983

Sir,
   I have the honour to report that I have today handed over the Army
under my command. To the best of my knowledge there are no
deficiencies to report, and the morale of all ranks is of a high order.
   I remain, Sir, your obedient servant.

General

15
Higher Training

A large and imposing building is the home of the senior Defence College in this country. It was originally founded after the First World War with a small number of students (or 'Members' as they are still called), military and civilian, to study the problems of the defence of the Empire, and appropriately was called the Imperial Defence College (or IDC). Over the years the number of Members has increased and by 1970, when I attended the one-year course, they comprised the United Kingdom, Commonwealth and NATO. The name was changed in 1971 to the Royal College of Defence Studies, and I was appointed Commandant 1983-84. By then the membership had increased to nearly 80 and included countries which were not members of the Atlantic Alliance (for example Brazil, Finland, Israel and Yugoslavia, to mention but a few).

In my judgement it is widely recognised as the most prestigious Defence College in the world and does more for British influence worldwide than any other institution or activity, with the exceptions of the Royal Family and the BBC World Service.

These jottings record only the humorous or the bizarre. The standard of debate and discussion in the College is extremely high, and in such respect is it held internationally that it attracts speakers of distinction from all professions world wide. 'No other country could possibly begin to run a college or a course like yours,' I was once told by a foreign ambassador. 'There is a unique and relaxed atmosphere here which makes those who wear the College tie feel that they are members of a select and elite club.' How right he was, and long may it continue so.

A COLLEGE VIGNETTE

The reply to a Member of the Imperial Defence College who asked a friend why he never said anything or questioned a lecturer, was that the friend could never think of anything to say.

'Well, if you do today I'll stand you a drink before lunch—or even two,' and he reminded him of this when the Course re-assembled after the break.

'Right,' said the Commandant, 'comments or questions, please.'

Deathly hush, until the friend rose and said to the erudite lecturer: 'Sir, I have understood .05 per cent of what you said this morning . . .'

'Don't be so conceited,' remarked the Member from the back. Both were subsequently reprimanded for being facetious.

THE PORTER'S REMARKS

The College curriculum allowed plenty of time for extra-mural studies, and by and large only the morning lecture was compulsory. Mr Smith, the Hall Porter, was a 'character', and when one Member's children came to collect their father at 3 p.m. and enquired of Mr Smith his whereabouts, he replied:

'My dears, I've been here many years. I've seen them come and go. Let me tell you, of all the Members I have seen, your Dad is the idlest. Catch him here after lunch? Not likely!'

And to another Member who later became the Chief of Staff of his Service whom he observed slipping past *before* lunch:

'Goodnight, sir.'

THE HAZARDS OF 'ABROAD'

An important (and popular) feature of the IDC and RCDS course was (and is) the overseas tour.

A Rear Admiral and I were accommodated, during a visit to Norway, in a students' hostel outside Oslo, which was bad enough. It was, moreover, 'dry', which made life so insufferable that we decided to go into town. We discovered a local train ran frequently and accordingly embarked.

'How will we get back?' I asked.

'Same way,' replied my friend.

'But how will we know where to get off? I've forgotten the name of the station.'

'Good point,' said the sailor. 'Leave it to me.' He went up to the Norwegian train guard and said to him very loudly, 'Pray tell me, my good man, I'm a British Admiral. Where have I come from?'

A group of Members from the Royal College of Defence Studies visit Stirling Castle as part of their tour of Scotland. An Israeli Colonel was so moved by the piper during lunch in the Mess of the Argyll and Sutherland Highlanders that he almost applied for transfer.

189

A BLACKPOOL INCIDENT

Curiously this particular 'overseas' tour began with two weeks spent in England and Scotland, and included in the former was a visit to Blackpool. The group even went up the famous tower, and one Member, in an attempt to get into the right mood, was seen emerging from the exit eating an ice-cream cornet and wearing a paper cap which read on the front, 'Kiss me Quick', and on the back, 'Cuddle me Closer'.

The senior Member drew him on one side and said, 'I don't think you should do that, you know. It give the Overseas Members a bad impression of the British Army!'

THE GROOVY GUNMAN

Members were told to write a thesis of 20,000 words. I was not sure what a thesis was and had to look it up in a dictionary, and anyhow could think of nothing I wanted to write about. A list of 150 suggested subjects was put up on the board, and with reluctance I chose 'The Generation Gap'—after all, I had five children, and several grandchildren who thought me pretty square. They also thought me idle when they called at Seaford House and saw keen fellow Members bent over books and papers in the Library, but not me. I promised them that I would apply my mind to it all in due course, and I even visited my tutor who was a Professor of Sociology in Bradford.

Leave came and we repaired to the Isle of Wight where I had a stroke of luck. 'Fiery Creations' were about to hold a Pop Festival which in the event was attended by three times the total population of the island and twice the strength of the entire Army. I attached myself to the hippy commune (almost certainly the first time in history such a thing had been done by a Guards Brigadier), the members of which, not suprisingly, asked what I was. I said I was a student (which was true).

'Of what?' they asked.

'War,' I replied, and as a result I was called 'The Gunman'. As they got to know me better, I became 'The Groovy Gunman', and ended with the accolade of 'Old Groovy'.

Occasionally I worked in the Medical Centre—in a clerical capacity. My job was to record the personal details of those who wanted to see the doctor—an elementary and somewhat lowly task, it might be thought, but it had its moments. For example:

'Name and particulars, please?' I asked a Flower Child, as some called themselves, and the reply was, 'I am a Child of the Universe.'

'Sorry, chum, unless you say that you are P. Snooks of 6, Lower Totland Road, Skipton, or wherever, you won't be allowed in.' This advice was not always well received by the applicant.

My thesis *was* well received by the Commandant, who was impressed by my tutor's high commendation. 'A first class piece of original research,' he had written—but mind you *he* had never been to a Pop Festival; nor, for that matter, had the Commandant.

A MEMBER'S SUGGESTION

The College visited Shell, a most interesting and valuable annual event. During the course of the day, I said to a distinguished overseas Member, 'Why don't you ask a question? Oil is a very important subject affecting us all, you know.'

The Member replied, 'I realise that, but the only question I can think of is, "Why are we visiting Shell and not BP?" '

'I don't think that would be very tactful,' I said.

'Oh, I would tell them that you had suggested I should ask it!'

THE PRAYER

I was touring Burma with a group of Members and when visiting a temple was invited to place a piece of gold leaf on the head of the extremely large statue of the Lord Buddha. This was a signal honour. As we climbed to the top, the priest asked if, by chance, I was a Buddhist.

'Surprisingly, I am not,' I replied.

'Well,' said the priest (and by this time we had reached the top), 'if it upsets you doing this, as you place the leaf, pray for Queen Victoria.'

THE FOREIGN MINISTER

I and my group of Members on an overseas tour had a private meeting with the Foreign Minister of a country that was so non-aligned it had left the Non-Aligned Movement. Right from the start it was plain that the Minister was ill at ease, so much so that he was trembling and reluctant to speak. Whether this was due to the charismatic personalities of the visitors or to the fact that three officials were present and four female stenographers, who recorded every word, was not clear, but the meeting was not productive; an effort was demanded to liven things up.

'Your Excellency,' I said, 'I have met many distinguished men in my time—and women, too, but you are unique. I have met no one who has been Ambassador in the capitals of both super-powers. If there is anyone who is able to predict a possible change in their relationship you are that person. What, sir, is your view?'

There was a shattering silence, and the Minister looked more miserable than ever. The girls gazed at him, pencils poised. After what seemed a very long time, he braced himself and said, 'They may go up or down, left or right,' and stopped.

I riposted, 'Amazing! And, Your Excellency, following that

Glasnost in Bulgaria . . .

extremely perceptive analysis, might I ask a further question? This remarkable change that you mention: do you think it will happen in my lifetime, or that of my children or, perhaps in that of my grandchildren?'

The Minister thought hard and long, clasped his hands and eventually replied, 'Possibly.' I realised I had to admit defeat and said goodbye.

Two days later the Ambassador, with whom I was staying, held a dinner party and produced the seating plan. To my horror and dismay I saw that my neighbour was the Minister and I anticipated a catastrophic evening. How wrong I was. Without

193

his officials and stenographers, the Minister was a changed man: he never stopped talking, was witty, provocative and even *risqué*! Life is full of the unexpected.

AN INDIAN INCIDENT

On that same tour we visited New Delhi, where we were to be briefed by the Minister of Home Affairs. Accordingly we were ushered in to the Briefing Room in the Ministry and, shortly after, a distinguished-looking Indian entered the room. As was my wont on these occasions, I shook him warmly by the hand.

'Very nice to see you, and good of you to spare the time. Let me introduce the Members of my College—they have all been specially selected by their respective Governments to attend the course and are destined for higher things'—and they were presented one by one. Inwardly I confessed to slight surprise when a look crossed the Indian's face which indicated a degree of astonishment, and I was taken aback when he then left the room. He reappeared two minutes later with a tray of refreshments and biscuits. He was not the Minister: he was the charwallah!

A SOCIAL GAFFE

As Commandant, I was invited to dine at an annual gathering in a public school, the object of which was to enable the dons and members of the Sixth Form to meet distinguished men and women from varying walks of life.

I was sitting opposite a man who turned out to be a Senior Civil Servant, and later on in the meal the conversation turned to the Royal College of Defence Studies.

'You know,' I said, 'you are just the sort of chap who ought to come and lecture at Seaford House.'

'I do,' came the reply.

'Oh, really, on a casual basis?'

'No, I come every year.'

An awful thought entered my head: 'Have you been this year?'

Answer: 'Yes.' My fears were sharpened.

'But was I there, introduced you and summed up at the end?'

'Do you know,' replied the Civil Servant, 'I can't remember.'

Touché.

ITALIAN (AND COMMONWEALTH) HISTORY

A very senior official of the Commonwealth Secretariat in Marlborough House came to Seaford House to lecture about the Commonwealth. During the question period, he was asked when his Secretariat had been formed, and he had to admit that he did not know. The Italian Army Member at once rose and gave the date, much to the delight of his colleagues.

Later I congratulated him on his knowledge, but added, 'Just remind me: when did Garibaldi die?' A look of horror crossed the Italian's face. He did not know! 'Well, never mind. I can't recall, off-hand, when he was born.' Horror! He did not know that either!

The next morning, on my arrival, I was met by the Italian with the answers, and before introducing the Lecturer of the day, I said to the Members:

'You may recall that our Italian colleague knew the date when the Commonwealth Secretariat was formed. The dates of birth and death of Garibaldi temporarily eluded him, when I sought to refresh my memory, but naturally he quickly was able to

195

remember. What he does *not* know, however, is this: when Garibaldi visited this country for the first time, he went to the Isle of Wight, a centre of Liberalism, and stayed in the home of my wife's Great-Great-Grandfather. Indeed, he planted a tree there to mark the occasion. My wife's Great-Great-Grandmother immediately fell madly, but secretly, in love with the Great Patriot, and "acquired" one of his handkerchiefs which, for the rest of her life, she kept beneath her pillow.'

The Italian Member was deeply moved, gratified by this intelligence—and made a note!

THE BOOK

A famous TV personality came to dinner, and over the port he asked me, 'What do you think of such-and-such a book?'

My reply was that I had not read it.

'Haven't read it? What do you mean "Haven't read it"? You, the Head of the most prestigious Defence College in the world and the Senior General in the British Army. Why haven't you read it?'

'Well', I said, 'there is a limit to the capacity of the human brain. You've written a book, haven't you? I haven't read that either.' The guest was crushed, but only momentarily!

A NAVAL OCCASION

The College regularly visits the Royal Navy and on one occasion I was allotted a young Marine to show me round HMS *Victory*. When at last we arrived at the spot where Lord Nelson died, the guide said:

'And 'ere 'is Lordship expired and every member of the fleet was sad 'cos he was an 'ero. "Bury me at 'ome, 'Ardy," were 'is Lordship's last words. This caused a problem because England was some way off in sailing time, but the Royal Navy rallied round: they popped 'im in a barrel and filled it up with rum. When they got 'ome, 'is Lordship was in prime condition. The lads didn't want to see the rum go to waste so they toasted their 'ero, and *that*, sir, is the origin of the expression "full bodied".'

THE COUNTER DEMO

A 'Ban the Bomb' procession wended its way interminably through the square. I stood on the pavement with my dog, waiting to cross and enter the square gardens. The latter became increasingly restless; the former decided some positive action was imperative. I had a loud voice and shouted:

'Stop! Death to the Imperialist Fascists! Long live the Soviet Union! Keep SS20!'

The procession stopped, dumbfounded, and I and my dog crossed unimpeded to our destination.

PARKER, PARKER & PARKER, Solicitors,

42 PORTMAN SQUARE, LONDON W.1.

Sir,

The members of the Noise Abatement Society of Great Britain resident in Groom Place, S.W.1. have ordered me to give notice that any recurrence of that hideous cacophony heard recently in the early morning emanating from a person unknown, male or female, wearing short skirt, will give rise to proceedings for damages.

It is understood that the noise purported to represent a Celtic nobleman leaving his domain.

Yours faithfully,

N. O. Sey-Parker

General Sir Michael Gow,
Seaford House,
37 Belgrave Square,
London S.W.1.

FELICITOUS TURNS OF PHRASE ON THE MIDDLE EAST

'There is no situation in the Middle East that is so bad that it cannot get worse.'

'The Iranian Government has been relatively strict on drug dealers—they execute them.'

RANDOM REMARKS

The lecture was one of the worst of the year.
First Member: 'This chap is a lecturer at Jesus College, Oxford.'
Second Member: 'Funny, I thought he was an anaesthetist.'

Lecturer talking about extraction of minerals: 'The sea bed has been very slow to get off the ground.'

On language problems in India: 'There are 14 recognised languages but Hindi is the official one. Unfortunately, to the people in the Southern States, Hindi is literally Greek!'

Overseas Member, in reply to a question about his forthcoming weekend activities: 'We are going to the Beating of the Troops.'

A BBC comment on ITV: 'Like the battleship *Potemkin*: too dependent on the ratings.'

Ex-Home Secretary: 'The Prison Service is riddled with restrictive practices.'

A visiting foreign diplomat:

'When I was asked to give this talk, I was asked if I minded questions, and of course I said no. Now I see you expect answers as well!'

'If, by the end of this talk, you have a clear, balanced and well formed view of the issues, then I have totally failed to convey the realities of the situation.'

Member to lecturer: 'I realise that the question I am about to ask is completely impossible to answer.'
Lecturer: 'Don't underestimate me, sir!'

To the Commandant of the National Defence College, New Delhi: 'The trouble with hierarchical systems is that there are too many chiefs and not enough Indians.'

16
Towards the End of La Vie Militaire

THE ABSENT-MINDED GENERAL

I was now nearing retirement. I had always wanted to visit the RAF College Cranwell, and this was arranged specially for me. The programme was so interesting that inevitably we ran behind time, arriving ten minutes late for lunch in the Mess. I handed my hat to a civilian Mess servant.

'How long have you been here?' I asked.

'Thirty-three years,' was the reply.

'Marvellous. It's men like you who maintain traditions and standards.'

I was hurried in to lunch, which was excellent, but we were now 20 minutes behind schedule. On departure, I thought I must thank someone, and warmly shook the hand of a man by the door.

'I *did* enjoy that. Your Messes are so well run. How long have you been here?'

'Thirty-three years, and 40 minutes since you last asked me that question,' he replied.

THE FALL

I was the only serving soldier to have fallen at Waterloo, which delighted the media as I also happened to be the Senior General in the Army. It occurred on Platform 6 of the London Railway Terminus.

Two months later, I returned and boarded the train which, had I survived, I *would* have travelled on. Looking at the five occupants of the compartment, absorbed, exhausted commuters, embedded as usual in their newspapers, I was suddenly seized with—who can tell what?:

'Listen to this,' I announced. Down came the papers, and astonishment, dismay, even fear filled their eyes. (Who or what is this lunatic?) 'Two months ago I fell on the platform—just there. Get up and look. There I lay for 40 minutes with every bone in my foot broken and the limb facing backwards, in biting cold, waiting for an ambulance . . . I expect they'll put a plaque up . . . I hope nothing awful happens now.'

" 'No. 273. General Sir Archibald' — why it's me!" Cartoon by Osbert Lancaster from *Tableaux Vivants. Reproduced by permission of The Estate of Sir Osbert Lancaster and John Murray (Publishers) Ltd*

A small man in the corner quaked, whereupon the station announcer said, 'We regret the delay in the departure of the train on Platform 6. This is because the driver has not arrived.'

'There you are,' I cried. 'What did I tell you?'—and pointing to the corner cringer I added, 'Don't get out, you might fall down.'

A MEDICAL BOARD

As I lay in bed in hospital, recovering from this fall, I kept receiving messages from the Military Secretary's Department about my progress. I felt gratified that the Military Secretary was being so solicitous and expected any day to receive a gift from the members of the Army Board of fruit, flowers and whisky. I waited, however, in vain, and received instead a message saying that the Regulations dictated that I could not be retired from the Army while I was in hospital; as I was already the oldest member of the Armed Forces and almost 'Senior Citizen Status', it was thought only a matter of time before there would be Questions in the House as to how much longer I would remain on the Active List.

The temptation crossed my mind that perhaps I could extend my Service till I was 70—after all, in the Soviet Union they had Generals older than that—but I did not want to overdo it. So I allowed myself to be discharged, and in due course was summoned to appear before a Medical Board, the Head of which was a charming doctor, even older than me.

'Come and sit down,' he said, 'you seem to have a terrible lot wrong with you. We'd better start with your hearing and . . .' At that moment his assistant coughed.

'I'm awfully sorry, but I didn't catch what you said.'

'My word,' he remarked, 'you really are deaf.' And he shouted, 'Tanks or Artillery?'

'Both,' I replied.

203

'Right, now the next thing is sight. This doesn't look too good, either. Stand on that cross on the floor and tell me what you can read on the chart.'

Readers may not believe me, but it *is* true. I saw the cross, upon which I stood. I looked round the walls, which were covered in posters—'Do not drink', 'Smoking kills', etc., etc.

'Sorry, doctor, where is the chart?' I think he concluded that I was physically bad or mad or probably both. But I got a disability pension!

Wilderness House, Hampton Court. The Chief Steward's gift of Duart whisky, 61st birthday.

RESETTLEMENT PROBLEMS

My son had become an extremely successful Management Consultant, or 'Headhunter', and so I thought it only sensible that I should consult him about future convivial and, perhaps, lucrative employment.

As one gets old, fact and fiction tend to become inextricably muddled in one's mind, so that it is difficult to distinguish between events that might have happened and those that in fact did. I am not entirely sure into which category the following falls.

'The trouble with you,' he remarked, 'is that you don't project yourself well; you're too modest.'

'I thought that was rather a good thing,' I replied.

'Not really. Just let's imagine that you are being interviewed. Who are you? . . . Go on, what would you say?'

'Well, I suppose I'd say that I was just an old general.'

'That's absolutely useless,' he said. 'That won't get you anywhere. What you must say is that you commanded three quarters of a million men and were responsible for a capital investment of over £8 billion.'

'Good heavens! Was I really?'

'Of course you were! If you had burnt down all the barracks and lost all the tanks, just think . . . and that's just for starters.'

'But whatever would I want to do that for?' I asked.

'Oh, you really are hopeless!' my son retorted. 'You'd better write out your curriculum vitae, send it to me and we'll see what we can do.'

And so I did, only to be told that there were two spelling mistakes in it. And that is why, I suppose, I still remain:

General (retired)

Postscript

These have been jottings from the past, but I end on a more serious note for the future:

There was a boy at public school who was an outstanding cricketer, as had been his father. Sadly, the latter had lost his sight, but he regularly came to the school whenever a match was played. Either his son sat beside him, or a friend, giving a ball by ball account.

The day his father died there was a major school match, and all the boys assumed that his son would be in no mood to play for the team, but to their surprise not only did he play but he made the highest score of the season.

'How could you go in and bat like that when your father was not here to see you?' he was asked.

'Oh,' he replied, 'but he *was* here, and for the first time was able to watch me play.'